What the Experts Are Saying about
The Art of Coaching Young Athletes

Coach Rick is unequalled at inspiring excellence in athletes and their teams. His words bathe youngsters in confidence and pride, emphasizing hard work, personal improvement, and respect for themselves and their teammates. The life skills he teaches will lead young people to success on the playing field and in life.

LORI BEDELL
Mother of three girls who were coached by Rick Peterson

The Art of Coaching Young Athletes is simply a gem! Rick Peterson's years of coaching children from their beginnings through the high school years provides the ideal roadmap on how to become a successful and motivating coach of young athletes. This book is a must for every age group coach who wants to further understand the practicalities and psychology of coaching our nation's youth.

TERI CONKLIN
Assistant Coach, New Trier Swim Club and parent of two young athletes

My two sons were fortunate enough to have had the opportunity to be coached and mentored by Rick Peterson over the span of a decade. Between them we participated in a multitude of sports, including soccer, basketball, baseball, football, hockey, tennis, water polo and swimming; some were at a highly competitive level, some were recreational. Both boys, without hesitation, would tell you that the best coach they ever had was Rick.

What makes Rick stand out above the rest is his ability to make even the most laborious workouts enjoyable; to create a sense of team even in a very individualized sport like competitive swimming; to use sincere positive reinforcement to motivate and teach. Each and every child knows that Rick is interested in their personal development and is internally motivated to do his or her best both for Rick and the good of the team.

The remarkable result of this positive coaching style is that it *works*.

Without yelling, humiliation, threats or punishment, his students learn, improve and excel. Not only have I witnessed non-swimmers become competent and water safe over a 6 week summer program, some of his athletes went on to be champions at state and national levels.

His philosophy and methodology of coaching should be must reading for anyone considering becoming a teacher or a coach.

LESLIE FARMER
Parent of two sons coached by Rick Peterson

If you want to become a good coach for your youth program, this book will help you accomplish that goal. If you already coach at the youth level and you want to improve your coaching skills, this book should become part of your library.

MARK G. GERVAIS
Wrestling coach (head coach 1983–2008), Marist High School, Chicago
Director of Greco-Roman Wrestling, Team Illinois

Coach Rick Peterson understands young people both as athletes and as developing individuals. In his coaching he communicates his belief in all team members, no matter what their ability levels. He offers constant encouragement by recognizing achievement and urging improvement. From Coach Peterson our three children learned the elements of athletic skill and competition, but more essentially they learned the principles of good sportsmanship and how to cooperate and contribute as members of a team. These are lessons for life.

MARY HENRY AND RICK MULLIN
Parents of three children who worked with Rick Peterson for many years.

The perfect antidote to the win-at-any-cost mentality of youth sports. A brilliant treatise for coaches on teaching teamwork, leadership, motivation and personal growth to kids, from kindergarten through high school.

DR. SUSAN KUCZMARSKI
Leadership Expert, Author, *The Sacred Flight of the Teenager:*
A Parent's Guide to Stepping Back and Letting Go,
Apples Are Square: Thinking Differently About Leadership

I had the distinct pleasure of watching Rick Peterson greatly impact my children's lives through his unique coaching style. Rick views each student as a whole person, knowing that a connection between their mental and physical abilities is essential in helping them reach their full athletic potential. Rick is systematic in developing skills, and using those skills as a building block to usher the student to the next level. All the while, mentally motivating children to reach within one's self to achieve individual goals.

Rick's has the most remarkable ability to acknowledge and nurture individual achievements which become stepping-stones for lifelong success. I have personally witnessed my children, who are now grown, apply these fundamental "Peterson Skills" to their personal, athletic and professional careers with great success.

Rick has a genuine gift as a coach, captured in these pages, will empower all that read this book to become a better coach, parent or employer. It reaches all those levels.

KATE SHAPIRO MS BA
Director/Owner Kid-Motion, Inc.

The Art of Coaching Young Athletes

RICK PETERSON
Foreword by PETER N. KOZURA

Racom Communications
Urban Heritage Press

Editor: Richard Hagle
Cover and interior design by Sans Serif, Inc., Saline, MI

Published by:
Racom Books/Racom Communications
Urban Heritage Press
150 N. Michigan Ave. Suite 2800
Chicago, IL 60601
312-494-0100/800-247-6553
www.racombooks.com

ISBN: 978-1-933199-29-0

Contents

Foreword

When I was asked to write a foreword for Rick Peterson's book, I was somewhat taken aback, albeit positively. I had never written, or been asked, to write a foreword or testimonial for someone, so I took this request extremely seriously and with honor and respect.

Although I do not have a background as a competitive swimmer, athletics has played a major role in my life, both from a competitive standpoint, as well as from a career standpoint. I grew up playing virtually every sport. I was fortunate enough to excel in baseball, which helped me immensely in understanding many life skills which I utilize to this day. In fact, through baseball I was able to attend an Ivy League institution- Cornell University and continue my baseball career, but, more important, continue my academic pursuits.

My professional career has been involved in sports as well. I have worked in the front office of a professional soccer team, directed the Chicago Marathon for a number of years, managed the operations of an auto racing facility, and now am the Executive Director of Illinois Swimming—a local Swim Committee of USA Swimming. Throughout my athletic and professional careers I have been in close contact with numerous coaches and managers. Truthfully, I have played under the tutelage of what I would consider some great coaches and also under some poor ones. But I can honestly say I have never seen a coach with as much enthusiasm and passion for his athletes' success as Rick. As I read his manuscript, I could also see his passion and enthusiasm for sharing a career of coaching knowledge with others. His philosophy of coaching, and the path to success for a coach and his athletes that he has written about, is applicable to all youth sports. Coaches are among the most influential adults in the lives of youth athletes. They are key to developing character in our children and sports provides the perfect environment for teaching life lessons.

After reading this book, you will take away a number of meaningful guidelines to becoming a successful and respected coach. Among them are the guidelines for coaching competency, the commitment to excellence (both on and off the field of play), your commitment to constantly developing your own skills, and the willingness to collaborate and share your successes with other coaches. Your on-field guidelines will include your paramount concern for the health and safety of your athletes, a focus on mastering skills (rather than solely on winning and valuing teamwork), and providing support for your athletes. Your off-field guidelines will focus on the development of your athlete as a person rather than just his or her athletic prowess and your understanding of your role as mentor and role model. Lastly, Rick addresses respect for all teammates, opponents, and officials, upholding the spirit as well as the rules of the game and a love of the particular sport that you are involved in. Whether your passion, desire, commitment, and dedication take you to the baseball field, basketball court, soccer field or swimming pool, this book will certainly help you on the way to becoming the type of coach every athlete would like to compete for. Enjoy!!!!

PETER N. KOZURA
Executive Director, Illinois Swimming
a Local Committee of USA Swimming

Acknowledgments

The seeds that ultimately grew into this book were planted early in my coaching career. Since early in my career I have been fortunate to have coached many sports, and in one sport (swimming) to have coached all ages at virtually every skill level. I first put pen to paper more than 25 years ago, and 1 still amazed by how long it has taken me to put these thoughts together. I am forever thankful to Julianne Carroll, fellow child development enthusiast, who helped me get this project off the ground. Through discussions and the reviewing of my early work, she was instrumental in my visualizing, then tackling and streamlining, this project. Others who helped me work through the issues in this book and/or reviewed and improved many of the chapter rough drafts include: Kate Shapiro, Mary Henry, Lori Bedell, Jennifer Guy, and Fritzi Soutsos.

Since this project's inception, my family has been amazingly supportive and understanding of my efforts. Thank you Sandy, for supporting my passion for this project, and thanks so much Elizabeth, Ian, and Sarah for cheering me on all these years!

A huge thanks must go out to Dan Spinella, who took the rough drafts and made them more connected and readable. In essence, he performed the miracle of taking the pieces and ingredients I fed him and whipping them into a coherent whole.

As this project has neared the finish line, I have had nothing but help and support from my wonderful publisher, Rich Hagle, who has been one of the easiest professionals to work with I have ever encountered. I am fortunate that this book has come under Rich's protective wing.

And then there is the "quarterback" of this project, Graham Hawkes, who has been indispensable in shepherding the project through the fog of presenting it to publishers, selecting the best one for the book, connecting me with indispensable Dan, and in lending his time, advise, and unwavering enthusiasm over the last several years to seeing this thing through to the finish.

The Attainable Coaching Experience

Coaching can be one of the most enjoyable and rewarding pursuits. As a coach, you can experience a wonderful sense of life purpose and accomplishment: the thrill of helping engineer and witnessing great performances; the challenge and strategy involved in contests; the trips, adventures, and extraordinary experiences; the countless connections with athletes, fellow coaches, parents, officials, and others, many blossoming into great and lasting friendships. Underpinning everything is the satisfaction gained by helping young people develop in both their respective sports and their lives. That, in a nutshell, is the amazing, attainable coaching experience.

And it's not just for the pros. A significant percentage of Americans will spend time coaching, either as volunteers or as professionals, at some point during their lifetimes. The vast majority of those experiences will occur in age group sports, also known as *youth sports,* which cover roughly ages five through eighteen or the kindergarten through high school years.

How and why do we become coaches? In ways almost too numerous to count. Perhaps the head coach of your daughter's youth soccer team is looking for an assistant. Or a local PTA board member implores you to do your duty for school and community. Maybe a friend or former teammate gives you a call and asks for your help. Or maybe you were really good at a particular sport in high school or college and want to pass on what you have learned to the next generation. Or maybe you just enjoy working with people. I was a teenager when I got my start. My summer swim coach asked if I would help out with the youngest team members. At the expense of being repetitive: The reasons for entering the coaching ranks are endless.

Incidentally, a great athlete does not necessarily a skilled coach make. On the other hand, a not-so-hot athlete can make a fabulous coach. Much more important than one's athletic achievements are (1) powers of observation; (2) the ability to connect with others; and (3) the ability to motivate. So take heart! It is possible to excel as a coach no matter what your background.

So now, for whatever reason, you find yourself a coach of young athletes. What do you do now?

No matter what your experience level (whether as a Little League prodigy or an armchair coach at home in front of the TV), you need to understand one fundamental idea: Coaching age group athletes is very different from the coaching of college or professional athletes and that the younger the athletes, the more this is true. Actually, it's best to think of age group coach as its own distinct, unique position. You'll be able to find this unique balance if you ask yourself the following questions:

- How should I treat these children?

- Why are these children in my program? To learn the sport? To get into or maintain a certain level of fitness? To have fun and make friends? To shoot for the stars?

- Are they beginners or more advanced?

- Should I be tough or easygoing? When and how?

- Should I have a lot of rules? What kind?

- What role should parents have in this program?

- Am I a teacher? A disciplinarian? A babysitter? A friend?

The fact is, for the vast majority of novice age group coaches, it's a baptism by fire. Very few receive any formal classes or other specific instruction before being thrown in the deep end. The questions above will help you define your purpose(s) and goals as a coach and help you reach them with a solid plan of action and conduct.

This chapter will define coaching, compare and contrast it with teaching, and explore what makes coaching in general and coaching age groupers in particular an art form. For there are some coaches—and you may have seen them—who are truly exceptional at their craft. Indeed, they work so effectively and with such authority, ease, and passion that we say they are practicing the *art of coaching*.

Defining Coaching

The *American Heritage Dictionary* (2nd college ed.) defines a *coach* as "a person who trains athletes or athletic teams." *Merriam-Webster* (3rd ed.) says a coach is "a private tutor [as well as] one who instructs or trains a team of performers."

In other words, a coach works with athletes, singly or in groups or teams. (Note: In our contemporary world, we have voice coaches, positive mental attitude coaches, and so on. They all share similar traits with sports coaching, but for the purpose of this book, we will be focusing on the coaching of athletes.) What is more, the words *train* or *training*, which appear in both definitions, point to the coach's main objective, which is the improvement of his or her athletes, as in "to make proficient with specialized instruction and practice" (*American Heritage Dictionary*). Combine these definitions with our earlier observations, and we now have a basic idea of what a coach is.

- A coach is knowledgeable about his/her sport.
- Coaching can be done one-on-one or with groups or teams.
- Coaching involves instruction and training, with greater proficiency as the objective.
- The coach is the leader, ultimately responsible for all decisions affecting the group.

Now let us expand our understanding of coaching by comparing it with teaching.

"Coaching is Teaching"

John Wooden, the legendary UCLA men's basketball coach, widely regarded as one of the greatest coaches ever in any sport, once said, "Coaching is teaching." Those three words capture a fundamental truth about what our profession should be all about. We are teachers whose classrooms happen to be ball fields, rinks, courts, and pools. So let's look more closely at the four basic elements common to both teaching and coaching, thereby recognizing the similarities and differences and identifying how both teachers and coaches can become more effective by becoming more like the other.

1. Education/Instruction

Whether it is a biology student attempting to understand photosynthesis or a wrestler struggling to master the rudiments of the single-leg take-down, the pupil must gain the necessary knowledge to become more accomplished in a field. To be successful, both teacher and coach must be well versed in their subject and have the ability to communicate that knowledge effectively. True, classroom teaching generally involves more time spent formally instructing than does coaching. But for both, educating the youngster is the initial step toward improvement.

2. Motivation

At first glance, it would seem that only coaches need concern themselves with motivation. After all, isn't it the physical difficulty of lifting the weights, running the laps, or scrimmaging in 95-degree heat that conjures in our minds the *need* for motivation? We certainly don't hear shouts of "You can do it!" or "Just one more!" ring out in the history classroom! Because sports require so much physical effort, there is usually more overt motivation.

However, motivation comes in many forms, and both teacher and coach need to understand and be adept at motivating if the pupil-athlete lacks self-discipline, energy, effective habits, or desire. If the pupil-athlete does not *want* to improve, if there is no *motivation* to learn, or if he or she is distracted, that mind or body will just shut down and nothing much will penetrate. Therefore the need, at times and in both professions, to motivate. Remarkable teachers, like outstanding coaches, tend to inspire their charges to greater heights and often instill a permanent enthusiasm and even love for that subject or sport. And though efforts at motivation may be displayed more often and certainly more obviously in the sports world, it is an important portion of the equation in both professions.

3. Practice/Repetition

For the athlete it is called a workout, a drill, or a training session. For the student: study hall, homework, or memorization. Either way, this third component takes what one has learned and commits it to habit and memory—mentally, neuromuscularly, or both. A swimmer may learn how to do the butterfly stroke on a given day, but unless he or she practices the correct stroke technique over and over, that skill will erode and the stroke will collapse. Similarly, a geography student who learns the location of each of the fifty states are but never commits the location of the states to memory may not be able to locate a particular state in the future, should the need arise. Practice embeds the correct knowledge, or "way," into the brain and/or muscles and makes it *learned*, or *habit*. Additionally for the athlete, practice builds up the overall level of physical fitness.

4. Improvement

This is the goal of both teaching and coaching: to effect a positive change in the learner. Specifically, the goal is to help the youngster improve his or her knowledge, understanding, and application of the particular subject (biology, tennis). However, teachers and coaches have the opportunity to effect positive changes in their pupils in many other ways at the same time, such as improving the child's self-discipline, promoting success-oriented study and work habits (e.g., effective time management), and so on.

Comparing teaching and coaching is a great way to broaden our understanding of all that goes into being a coach. Also, recognizing all the similarities between coaching and teaching helps explode the image often associated with coaches, that all they do is blow a whistle and yell commands. A great coach is a great teacher. Both have an impact, a tremendously positive impact, on those they touch. They each instruct, motivate, and drill their charges in such a way that improvement, often major improvement, occurs. And a student or athlete's love for what is being taught often blossoms.

I am a firm believer that both professions would benefit a great deal by using the other's signature focus more often. Teachers should work more at inspiring their students, getting them excited, and spurring them on to greater intellectual heights, instead of taking for granted that their lectures and the writing on the blackboard are enough to plant that information permanently in the minds of their students. Conversely, many coaches would increase the speed, quality, and permanence of improvement in their athletes if they instructed more often and for a higher percentage of time, as opposed to just training them, often embedding bad habits instead of good in the process.

In any event, don't be fooled by the differences in subject matter (math versus lacrosse) or setting (indoor classroom versus outdoor field.) The coach's job, like that of a teacher, is to work with young minds and bodies, to convey expertise to them, and to galvanize them toward greater effort, the result being a vast improvement in their knowledge, capabilities, and accomplishments.

Why Have a Coach?

On a hot summer day, a child goes to the neighborhood pool and paddles around while having a good time with friends. She goes off the diving board and plays games like Sharks and Minnows and Tag—typical, normal fun in the water. However, if this child wants to improve her swimming skills, she will have to do some more difficult things, such as speed and stamina training and stroke technique work. If she works at it alone, she probably will progress somewhat. For instance, she can watch the techniques of other, superior swimmers and attempt to duplicate them, and she can swim more laps and try to go faster. But when we do things ourselves, there is a natural tendency to stop or pull back (often unconsciously) if things get too tough. And how in the world do we know if our technique is correct if we can't see ourselves!

Think about how much more quickly this girl will improve when a knowledgeable person sets the agenda and creates practices; when there is another pair of eyes telling her what she is doing right and wrong; and when that other person, that coach, continues encouraging her to aim higher, and praises her when she does. This scenario points out one of the critical reasons coaches exist and are so needed. *Coaches help people do what they would not normally do.* Granted, coaches teach and train athletes. But it's more than that. What are those athletes and teams doing? They are attempting to go *beyond the norm* in their chosen field. To truly understand the value of a coach, we need to understand that without a coach, anyone attempting to go beyond what's normal will have a tougher time accomplishing goals, and usually will not go as far. Using the earlier swimming example, ask any competitive swimmers—current or former— whether they gets more out of a practice if they are solo. The answer, of course, is an overwhelming "no."

Before we get too carried away, however, don't assume that all coaching is beneficial— that just by *being* a coach you are doing good. Truly bad coaches can often have an incredibly negative impact. At the extreme, a bad coach will psychologically tear down their athletes, preach hatred of the opposition, play favorites, or physically abuse his or her charges. Most insidious are the coaches who get positive results on the field at the expense of the overall mental and physical well being of the athletes. Coaches who say, "Winning is all that matters. Shut up and do as you're told!" fall into this category. I believe, however, that most inept coaching is due to ignorance—ignorance of the mental, psychological, and *human* aspects of coaching, not just the technical, knowledge-of-the-sport side. When you practice the art of coaching, you combine instruction, motivation, and training skills in such a way as to effect a positive change in your athletes both on the field and off. They will become better at their sport under your tutelage, and they will become better people.

The Art of Coaching

Coaching involves not only having knowledge of the discipline, but also the ability to instruct, motivate, and train your athletes to improve and succeed. The *art of coaching* involves the *blending* of these key aspects at the right time, in the right way. How do you train, instruct, and motivate? When? With whom? With what intensity? The variables can be innumerable. However, take heart! The novice coach *will improve steadily* by observing accomplished coaches, as well as by reading up on the subject, learning from one's own experiences, keenly observing the athletes, and most important, recognizing that coaching *is* an art, with innumerable factors and effective ways of doing things. In other words, there are often many best ways.

I was fresh out of college and a few weeks into my first year as a social studies teacher at New Trier West High School in Northfield, Illinois. I had signed on as an assistant coach with the school's age group swim program. Thus I found myself, one fine fall day, in Racine, Wisconsin, coaching at my first United States Swimming (U.S.S.) meet. As the warm-up session for the meet began, one of our best young swimmers asked me to look at his freestyle flip turn. Eric's turn certainly had some kinks in it, so we began to correct the glitches right then and there in the warm-up pool. In fact, after fifteen minutes we had achieved a miracle! His turn was now faster and far more efficiently. I congratulated myself on a great coaching job and anxiously awaited his 50-yard freestyle event. Two hours later, a psyched Eric launched himself off the block and looked sensational as he approached the turn. I eagerly anticipated seeing Eric's new smoother and quicker flip turn. He surged toward the wall, flipped, . . . and missed the wall! What a catastrophe! Well, he didn't actually miss the wall completely, his toe caught a piece of the edge. But Eric lost more than a second, and his overall time, which had appeared to be heading toward a personal record, sank instead to a second slower than his previous best. Needless to say, he was bummed, and so was I.

Later, as we reviewed the race, we both remained perplexed that our well-intentioned efforts had resulted in . . . *this*. What went wrong? Actually, in the name of coaching, I had violated what I later learned was a cardinal rule: Don't change anything that requires a change in muscle memory on game day. In other words, any physical change must become habit for it to be consistently successful. Eric had learned a better way, but because it had not become a habit, he actually fared far worse that day as a result. Good intentions plus terrible timing equaled lousy coaching or *over-coaching* (coaching when none is needed, or at the wrong place or time).

Over-coaching is one example of how the best of intentions can still result in failure. Learn from your successes *and* failures, learn from others, and don't forget to exploit your own unique strengths as you evolve as an increasingly more effective coach, for all humans have different strengths, weaknesses, and personality types. Therefore, there is no one perfect way for all coaches in all situations. Rather, each coach will have his or her own slightly unique style and method. An energetic, can't-sit-still coach might be hollering encouragement during a race, then bound over to the athlete afterward for a quick exchange of analysis and congratulations, while a quieter or more cerebral coach might simply observe the race, wait for the athlete to come over afterward, then quietly assess the performance—both with equal effectiveness and success.

Knowing there are many ways to achieve the same ends doesn't mean we don't continually attempt to find better ways to coach. My point is this: No one should count him- or herself out of becoming an effective coach just because of personality or background. Provided we have the right attitude and are willing to work hard, it is possible to become a reasonably effective coach. And as we learn more, not just about our sport but also about how to convey that knowledge, when to convey it, and with what kind of force or import, we will be well on our way toward becoming more skilled at our craft.

The Coach-Athlete Connection

There is one more aspect to the art of coaching, one more ingredient that may be overlooked but is often the key to effective coaching. *This single factor has more to do with coaching success than any other.* It is the *quality* of the connection between coach and athlete.

Think of the coach-athlete (C-A) connection as similar to that of an electrical connection. A high-quality electrical connection occurs when the cord is plugged in, the line is opened, and the lamp beams brightly. Something similar occurs when an athlete and his or her coach make a strong, positive connection. The athlete will try whatever the coach suggests because he or she respects and trusts that coach. A mediocre connection is like a lamp with the dimmer switch turned halfway down. There is still light, but not as much, as is the case with a mediocre C-A relationship (less communication, trust, and respect). And then there is the C-A relationship that is antagonistic or nonexistent. That situation is similar to pulling the plug—you have a very dark room indeed!

A quality connection allows information to flow through unimpeded—and be received willingly. And there is a recipe for high-quality connecting that is fairly easy to follow and incredibly rewarding for both parties. First, keep in mind that coaches have a jump start on this process.-We initiate the relationship, and therefore we have it in our power to be the architect of a strong, positive C-A connection.

What are the keys to building and sustaining a high-quality C-A connection?

1. **You care.** As a coach, you care about helping your athletes improve in your sport. You also care about their overall welfare and evolution as human beings. A truly caring coach is *invested* in his or her charges, willing to go the extra mile for them. As they come to understand this, athletes will tend to open up and be *guided willingly*. In fact, many of your athletes will want to please you as a direct result of your desire to help them.

2. **Enthusiasm.** You are passionate about your sport and excited about having the opportunity to help your athletes develop. They feel it, and tend to become more motivated.

3. **Respect.** All humans deserve respect—regardless of age. A common error committed by the first-time coach is to show the young athlete less respect than he or she would be accorded as an adult. When you first connect with athletes of any age, be sure to be polite, caring, and inquisitive about them, exactly as you would upon meeting an adult for the first time. And don't do any of the following: talk down to them, be sarcastic, demeaning, or in other ways make them feel *less than*. All athletes will respond more favorably to a respectful approach.

4. **It's about *them*, not you!**Is it more important that you see your name in the paper, or that the athlete does? Do you take most of the credit for the team's successes, or do you credit others? In the

movie *Varsity Blues*, the head coach, shooting for his tenth straight conference championship, plays some of his best athletes in the big game even though he knows they are seriously injured. "Shoot 'em up doc!" he barks to his trainer before game time, referring to the cortisone shots he wants administered to mask the pain. His players are mere pawns in his master plan to become the winningest coach in the league's history. Do *you* need personal glory to feed your ego? Do you need to be the star? If so, you are in the wrong business. Keep the spotlight on them. Your athletes will appreciate this and be drawn to your unpretentiousness.

5. **Trust.** A long-term, high-quality C-A relationship only grows stronger when your athletes see that you are *always* respectful, caring, and desirous of what's best, not only for the athlete, but also for each of their teammates as well. Consistency strengthens the trust that's been created. You would be amazed at what a few sarcastic remarks or other blatantly disrespectful words or actions can do to set back an otherwise strong working relationship. *Dis*trust tends to creep into the relationship. By keeping in mind the Golden Rule ("Do unto others . . ."), your relationships can only grow stronger.

The Coaching Experience

Coaching is hard work, particularly considering the sheer number of hours logged. However, the more focused effort you put into it, the more you accomplish, and the result is a hugely rewarding experience. There is simply a tremendous amount of satisfaction involved in developing young

---

The High-Quality Coaching Method

- Respectful, caring attitude toward, and connection with, *all* your athletes..
- Coaching objective is to help all your athletes reach their potential in that sport while helping them positively evolve in life.
- Instruction and motivation are accomplished through positive means, such as reason, creativity, and inspiration. A coach's objective is always to build up his/her athletes' skills, confidence, and self-image, not tear them down..
- Practices are varied, stimulating, challenging, interesting, upbeat. All are engaged.
- All actions by the coach reflect a goal of building a desire to excel *in* the athlete instead of imposing it *on* them.

athletes, not to mention a heck of a lot of fun too. The following are just a few of one's own desires and needs that are fulfilled by taking part in this occupation:

1. **Giving and Sharing.** Never forget that coaching is, first and foremost, for the children. We are there to help them, not just to fulfill our own grand designs or satisfy our own needs and wants. Having said that, one of the great things about coaching is that so often one can do both. For instance, when we become adults, there is often a part of ourselves that wants to give back to the people and institutions that helped us during our own formative years. My former situation is as good an example as any. In addition to coaching, I once traded U.S. Treasury note futures for a living for many years. Trading provided a comfortable living for my family and was a stimulating profession in its own right. However, though managing risk is a worthy occupation, especially in a vigorous, expanding world economy, trading didn't allow me to see or feel the kind of immediate, positive benefits I helped provide to others as a coach.

2. **Variety.** If you truly enjoy people and all the wondrous variations in their personalities and actions, there will never be a dull moment (except for some of the paperwork!). Each day is new and different and exciting, mainly because *people* are your focus and your "product," as opposed to things. Understanding your athletes' needs, moods, and motivations, and dealing with them every day is a constant challenge, as well as an ever-changing one.

3. **Leadership, Responsibility, and Control.** Many jobs involve having superiors whose orders you follow. Even in a great work environment, one can sometimes feel stifled, unheard, and frustrated by lack of advancement or recognition. As a lead coach, however, you are calling the shots and in control of your work environment; even as an assistant you are often in charge. Each day you put yourself on the line by being ultimately responsible for making the key decisions involving your group or team. Now I am *not* talking power trip here, where you go bossing everyone around just to feel superior. The power and control a coach has can be heady, so we can't lose sight of the responsibility that goes along with the position. Your decisions affect all the children under you and, by extension, their parents, so that poorly thought-out decisions or abuses of your position can have a major negative impact. That said, it's

pleasant to be working in an environment where one isn't constantly at the beck and call of others, where instead you are in control. And handling a position of leadership capably does wonders for one's self-confidence.

4. **Relationships.** If your coaching philosophy involves working with and understanding your athletes (as it should), and if you treat them and their parents with kindness and respect, then you will discover the great hidden bonus that participation in coaching brings—many wonderful relationships. It's simple arithmetic. The more athletes and parents you work with, the more marvelous associations you will develop. For instance, it's amazing and gratifying to me how many former pupils of mine are now adult friends, and that so many of their parents are great friends as well. It's not just because a coach spends so much time with the athletes. Rather, it's the *quality* of the relationships that is so special.

The athlete is grateful for all the help you have given, and that you are an adult who has believed in and treated him or her with respect. Parents, too, appreciate the way the coach has handled those who mean more to them than anything on this earth—their children. And of course you, the coach, are appreciative for having had the chance to develop this young person, as well as the support of their parents who've managed carpools, helping run contests, etc. Strong, positive bonds tend to develop. You have all worked toward the same goal—the improvement of the child in all ways.

This is the hidden bonus inherent in coaching—these great relationships that evolve during and after participation with your team. And the basis for all this? You, as a coach always striving to do right for your athletes. You seek to build them up, not tear them down. You have their interests at heart, recognize each as an individual, and truly care how they are doing, as athletes and as people.

▶ **Summary Points** ▶ ▶ ▶

▶ One can become a successful coach regardless of personality type or background, as long as the coach is always working for the betterment of the individuals under their tutelage.

▶ Coaching, like teaching, involves instruction, motivation, and practice, with the objective being improvement.

▶ The *art* of coaching involves the blending of the above aspects at the right time, in the right way.

▶ A high-quality coach-athlete (C-A) connection is the single most important factor in coaching success, and essential for a higher-quality experience for both athlete and coach.

▶ The keys to building and sustaining a high-quality C-A connection include—showing you genuinely *care* about the individual; showing enthusiasm, respect, and trust for the individual; and following the truism, "It's about *them*, not you!"

▶ The coaching experience is tremendously rewarding, satisfying, and fulfilling in so many ways, providing a hidden bonus—the development of many fantastic relationships, many of which will last a lifetime.

Motivation

Picture this: You are the coach of a team, but not just any team. This team's athletes can't wait to get to practice. They constantly pressure their parents to drive them to their workout. And early at that. Now flash forward. Your athletes have arrived at practice—eager, enthusiastic, clamoring to get going. You literally have to hold them back from taking the field before the previous group's time is up. Once they begin, the air is filled with excited yells and the sounds of a bunch of youngsters all totally into it. The next day this same group has a competition. Many of the spectators notice that this team's athletes seem so positive, focused, and energetic. They are cheering and supporting each other, alertly making plays, initiating conversations with their coaches about how they did and what they can do better, thoroughly enjoying the whole experience. This picture of a positive, motivated, indeed inspired group can be a reality you experience with your team.

Why do some people have energy and drive while others are listless? Why do some people lead lives of satisfaction and accomplishment while others seem stuck on a treadmill, no closer to their hopes and aspirations than before? Frequently, the answer is *motivation*, "the reason or cause that propels (humans) to action." W. Clement Stone, a foremost authority in this field, said, "A motive is an urge within an individual that incites him to action." The stronger the motive, the more powerful the response. Positive motivation is vital for achieving success and attaining personal fulfillment. It's also an essential ingredient in any high-quality age group sports program.

As I mentioned previously, motivation is one of the three main ingredients in coaching, along with instruction and training. In fact, motivation is often the major determinant in how much improvement will occur, for it is the degree of one's motivation that will decide whether one tends to settle for mediocrity or accomplish far more. However, certain motivational types and methods are of a higher quality than others. In general, internal (self-) motivation is the highest quality type, in part because the fires within burn continuously and therefore are in less need of periodic external "stoking." Yes, coaches should always work at inspiring their charges, but we should also help them develop the ability to motivate themselves through the teaching of goal setting, for instance, because, ultimately, that burning desire to succeed will be most consistently powerful if the impetus comes from inside. When our athletes develop the ability to motivate themselves, they discover the *power* to effect positive change in and outside sports throughout their lives.

There is a slew of methods coaches can use to motivate their athletes. A number of them are middling at best, and some are actually counterproductive. Keep in mind that *how* you move athletes, whether through fear or inspiration, will leave an imprint. For instance, certain methods can affect an athlete's progress immediately, yet have a negative impact on the individual down the road. With this information in mind, be careful to motivate with an eye on the longer-term ramifications of your actions.

The first objective of this chapter will be to list important factors to be aware of when rating motivational methods. Next, we will describe the main types of motivation and rate the relative quality and effectiveness of the methods coaches generally use. Then we will study the main driving motives characteristic of each age group's developmental level. Following that, we will explore specific motivational techniques coaches can use to help their athletes become self-, or desire-motivated, the highest form of motivation an athlete can attain. Finally, we will delve more deeply into goal setting, both individual and team.

Evaluating Motivation Methods

Perhaps the most critical distinction coaches make when deciding on a motivational method involves the effect of that method in the *short-term* (that second or minute or during that practice or contest) versus the *long-term* (weeks, months, years later). We often respond to a situation without thinking of how it will affect the athlete down the road. Sometimes it's because we care only about what's going on at that moment. But it may also be that we are oblivious to the ramifications our actions will have in the future. As coaches we should always be aware of the long-term ramifications of our methods, and choose and act accordingly.

Ideally, whatever motivational methods you use should positively impact the athlete both short- *and* long-term. However, especially when coaching age group athletes, *the long view is far more important than the achievement of immediate results.*

Short-Term Impact of Motivational Methods

The following are criteria coaches should consider when deciding if, when, and how one should employ certain motivational methods.

1. Effect on Performance

Most motivational methods can achieve short-term results. The question is, at what cost? Coaches often fall into the "results trap" by ignoring the fact that certain methods can carry excessive negative baggage. Since there are many methods at a coach's disposal in any given situation, part of the art of coaching is in discerning what to use when, so that the impact will be positive *in all ways as often as possible.* For instance, persuasion (reasoning) and inspiration are methods that often take longer and require more energy and patience than, say, yelling or threatening. Yet both the short- and long-term effect of persuasion and inspiration will generally be more positive. Therefore, it becomes more worthwhile to go the extra mile motivationally (use a higher level method) when we weigh both the short- and long-term ramifications.

2. Positive or Negative Delivery of Motivational Message

Are you being patient, supportive, encouraging, *positive*? Or are you angry, impatient, defensive, threatening, *and negative*? Does your motivational method help your athletes enjoy their practice or contest more than usual and/or derive greater satisfaction out of the effort and sacrifices they put in, or not? Your facial expressions (smiling vs. frowning, for instance), vocabulary, and the sound of your voice (tone and inflection) will all have a bearing on the quality of their experience that instant, that day.

3. "Have to" versus "Want to"

Does your motivational method prompt your athletes to want to join in a practice? Remember, there are many motivational types (e.g., "fear," "have to,", or "desire" motivation—see the "Hierarchy of Motivational Types" section), and you can have a huge impact on that question, no matter what the athlete's *current motivational type* may be at the time.

For example, let's say you have a wrestler on your team who is participating only to "letter," which will look good on his college applications. He may, in essence, be a closet "have to," and his lackadaisical efforts in workouts seem to bear this out. However, he also may be a possible key to victory in an upcoming match that looks to be nip and tuck on paper. You pull him aside a few days before the match and impress upon him the importance of his upcoming event. He buys into what you are saying, has great practices leading up to the big dual meet, and then pulls an incredible upset, helping the team to victory. Your motivational method was designed to create a "want to," and it succeeded. To take this example one step further, your success with turning a short-term "have to" into a "want to" may well have sparked the athlete to retain that "want to" attitude over a far longer period of time. For through the success he experienced, he may become far more excited about wrestling in general, and stop marking time merely to pick up a "letter".

4. Extrinsic versus Intrinsic Motivation

Is the athlete chiefly motivated from within, or intrinsically, which is generally more desirable (more dependable and longer lasting) than being motivated from outer, or external stimuli? The "want to" motivational types are mainly intrinsic in nature. That is, though some of the factors that influence the athlete are external (great teammates, inspiring coach), the athlete consciously decides she wants to succeed, so the fire comes mainly from within. Self-motivation, the highest form, is by definition intrinsic. The lower forms (fear, "have to", deception, and reward) are extrinsic in nature. The athlete is reacting to an external impetus (for instance, my parents want me to run cross-country, I don't) and not participating voluntarily. *Reward motivation* is an anomaly in that it is a "want to," but entirely extrinsic. It's a cheap form of "want to" because instead of the athlete deciding on her own to work harder, the external reward is the motivating force. Take away that extrinsic reward and motivation lags. Our objective should be to help our athletes become more intrinsically motivated.

Long-Term Impact of Motivational Methods

The following criteria speak more to the long-term impact of the various motivational methods we will discuss in the next section.

1. Love for the Sport

Does your method increase or decrease the athlete's desire to continue to be involved in the sport? Will the athlete continue, through the years, to want to improve? Will he or she continue to enjoy being involved? To a certain extent we are trying to make assumptions about the future that we won't be able to verify for years, so it might seem like a futile exercise to speculate on what this or that method will do to someone years down the line. However, we can form an educated guess as to each method's long-term effect. Fear-motivated athletes can't wait to get out of the sport, whereas desire-motivated athletes choose to be involved, making them more likely to continue.

By the way, let's acknowledge here and now that most athletes eventually reduce their involvement in a sport, or even leave the sport entirely, for reasons that are constructive. Sometimes their interests change, or they accomplish all they feel they can or want to. They also leave involuntarily, maybe after being cut and then deciding sports is just not of further interest to them. All are understandable, life-evolving reasons. But many athletes do burn out (leave voluntarily due to negative reasons), and often it's because of the thoughtless actions of their coaches. As you watch your athletes move on into high school, college, or even beyond—and even if they don't continue—be proud of the fact that so many benefited from and enjoyed their participation on—your team.

2. Self-Image Building

Are your motivational methods building the self-image of each of your athletes or harming it? This is an absolutely crucial question to answer honestly when one is involved in age group sports. These youngsters are often terribly uncertain about themselves. You have tremendous influence over them and can have a great impact on how they see themselves. Armed with the knowledge that children are still quite malleable and that their self-images are constantly evolving, one of your objectives should be to build the self-image of all your athletes. You can do this by pointing out when they improve, by helping them see the connection between their hard work and the resultant improvement, and by identifying and celebrating each athlete's unique contributions to the team. Your athletes will feel empowered, and their self-confidence will shoot skyward. Ultimately, they will feel more capable of doing *anything*. You are helping build the person, not just the athlete, and it may be the single greatest thing you can do for them.

3. Transferability of Lessons Learned

Many of the lessons learned through athletics are applicable to other areas of a person's life. Success habits we have previously discussed, such as time management and the relationship of hard work to success are transferable to areas such as school, business, and even one's personal life. Thus athletes can achieve greater success and have a higher quality of life if they are able to internalize these lessons and then transfer them to other areas. However, transferability is greatest when athletes are highly motivated. They aren't forced to learn, but rather desire to; as a result, they learn more and retain it better. Moreover, they experience success while going through the process, so they will be eager and able to use their knowledge to achieve success in other areas. However, if athletes dislike being involved in their sport, there often is a negative connotation attached to most anything associated with the activity. Sometimes burnout cases quit all sports due to such a negative connotation attached to those things inherent in all sports, such as discipline, sacrifice, practicing, and competition in general.

Hierarchy of Motivational Types

The following are common motivational types, listed from lowest- to highest-rated (in other words, from the least to most effective method based on the criteria used earlier) over the long-term. Keep in mind that a coach may use a lower-rated method that is as effective—for that minute, or even for that whole practice or contest—as one that is more highly rated. However, if you want to instill a lifelong love for your sport in the athletes you work with, the higher the form of motivation you use, the better chance you will succeed. Even more important, helping your athletes develop the ability to self-motivate in your sport helps them gain the ability to do so in other areas of their lives.

1. Motivation by Fear

This highly negative form occurs when athletes' actions are compelled by fear of the consequences should they not perform well. In rare cases athletes actually are terrified of the sport itself (for instance, divers whose anxiety about possibly hitting the board begins to color their entire experience), but more often athletes are afraid of their coaches' or parents' wrath or disappointment. The athletes' own internal fear of failure falls into this category as well. All motivation through fear focuses on the negative. The athlete feels he or she *has to* do well or suffer negative consequences.

Methods that induce fear include using coercion or intimidation, such as the use of physical or verbal threats. Often coaches will be oblivious to the fact that they are using fear motivation. Rather, they may rationalize that it's "just their style." Nevertheless, actions such as coaches screaming at their athletes, throwing objects, grabbing and shaking their players, and issuing ultimatums such as "do this, or else!" tend to instill anger and fear in athletes. These methods *may* have the desired impact *that instant,* but the long-term result is pain, disillusionment, lowered self-esteem, and a more negative outlook toward the sport. Therefore, if you are thinking at all of the bigger picture, use fear motivation only when absolutely necessary, such as in an emergency.

2. *The Unmotivated, "Have to" Athlete*

I rate this type of athlete higher in the hierarchy than Fear Motivation because the negative ("I have to participate, though I don't really want to") is not as profound as that in motivation through fear, and can more easily be turned to the positive. The unmotivated child has no desire to participate, but is required to, perhaps to satisfy a demand of his or her parents or to fulfill a school requirement. This type is your most common example of an unmotivated, or in some cases negatively motivated team member.

Parents select activities for their younger children for a number of reasons. Perhaps they see that the child may have some talent or likes the activity, or because other friends or schoolmates are participating—all great reasons. However, sometimes parents may err, by mistaking or ignoring their child's talent level or desires. Then they may insist that the child remain in the program long after any good can be gotten from participation in it. These actions can produce an unmotivated athlete.

A coach's attitude can also contribute to this situation. A coach's lack of interest or general negativity can help turn a motivated athlete into one whose spirit and effort crumble. Fortunately, a coach can often change an athlete from a "have to" to a "want to" merely by taking an interest in the child, attempting to understand him or her, and by helping him or her improve.

3. *Motivation by Deception*

This type of motivation occasionally crops up as a method used by coaches to squeeze that last bit of effort from the athletes, but it invariably leads to a reduction in trust by the athletes in their coach. Using this method, athletes will be told any- and everything, including exaggerations and even falsehoods, to induce emotion and performance.

For example, a coach saying, "This is the last sprint if it is done well" may initially cause athletes to try harder. However, if that is the first of ten sprints and the coach knows it, then in effect the coach was lying to the athletes. The stimulus is short-lived as everyone rapidly catches on, and worse yet, it leads to distrust and disillusionment with the coach, especially if the athlete feels he or she "did well" a number of times. Be a straight shooter—consistent in what you say and what you do.

4. Motivation by Reward

Using this method, coaches try to lure their athletes to perform by doling out promises, prizes, or other types of rewards ("Whoever makes ten straight free throws doesn't have to run laps"). It can be effective and enjoyable short-term, but motivation fails when the reward loses its value ("I already know I am a lousy free-throw shooter."). If used rarely, reward motivation can be fun, effective, and tosses some variety into the mix. However, this type of motivation should only be used in certain short-term situations and should be well thought out and planned in advance. Overuse of reward motivation results in athletes' coming to rely on some external force or lure to fire them up. Also, the move itself can fall flat.

Take the example of a coach who declares "Whoever wins this sprint gets out of practice early!" Well, what if everyone knows Sarah is the fastest? What incentive do the other athletes have to try? Of greater concern is the misuse of this method—say, when a coach uses "getting out of practice early" as a reward. This directly contradicts the coach's goal of building a love for the sport and desire for working longer and/or harder to achieve success! Now in rare cases, say when your football team is worn down and could use some rest and recovery, a "do this and we *all* can go home" can work. But be careful with reward motivation; use it sparingly and be cognizant of the underlying message you may be sending. And parents—if you notice that you are constantly bribing your child to attend practice, take that as a red flag and at least review what's going on with that child, and, in some cases, determine whether your child should continue in that activity.

The last three motivational types fall under the category of "want to", or "desire" motivation. The increase in desire within the category is one of degree. *The higher the degree of internal fire, as opposed to external factors driving the athlete, the higher the motivational type.* Self-motivation is the highest form of desire motivation because individuals choose to seize control of their own destiny. No one has to tell them to be at practice. They *choose* to improve and succeed. Yes, there are always a certain amount of other factors that play a part in athletes' overall motivation. However, instead of being major, or the major motivating factors, external stimuli such as team traditions, pleasing a coach, etc., merely feed athletes' internal hunger to be the best. For whatever combination of reasons individuals are powerfully, positively energized to succeed, and the impetus for their actions originate from within.

5. *"Want to" Motivation: Desire to Please Others*

Wanting to please someone is rarely the only motive at work, but it can be a large part of the overall motivational picture. Age group athletes especially have a powerful urge to please, whether it is a favorite coach, their parents, or some other significant figure. Some hero worship also may be involved, perhaps of a coach, teammate, or celebrated sports star. Acceptance by the peer group, an especially strong motivating factor with teenagers, offers another reason as to why the athlete may strive so hard. Short- and medium-term, the desire to please can be a powerful impelling force. However, it will tend to weaken once that key figure or group loses its significance, or when the desire or need to impress recedes.

The vast majority of humans have at least some desire to please others. If just for this reason alone, it is *so* important for coaches to take an interest in each athlete, to be positive and enthusiastic regarding the sport, and to be a positive role model. Athletes will want to perform better for such a coach. How you conduct yourself will go a long way toward capturing and firing up your athletes' interest. And through your continued encouragement and attention, you can often move the athlete from wanting to please *you,* to loving and embracing the sport itself.

6. *"Want To" Motivation:The Sport or Your Program (or both) are Fun, Interesting, Important*

Interest in the sport and/or your particular program is a more stable and longer lasting form of desire motivation. These athletes may respond to the unique rules, strategy, and intricacies of that particular sport. In addition, athletes may be inspired by the way you run your program. They may enjoy how practices are constructed and operated, as well as the great connection they may have with the coaching staff. Perhaps, the team's long tradition of success may be inspirational. In addition, athletes can be motivated by their status on the team, or instead be moved more by the "fun stuff", such as teambuilding outings. The list of possible motivating factors is endless.

As a coach you can make membership on your team or program desirable. Keep things fresh, varied, and stimulating. Focus your athletes on improvement. Keep all engaged and challenged. Make the working environment comfortable yet stimulating.

The summer swim team I recently coached may be somewhat radical in that we did not have minimum practice attendance requirements, either for membership on the team or for participation in meets. Yet attendance was excellent. What we tried to do was send the message loud and clear that improvement would occur, and at an accelerated rate, the more often the athletes attended. In addition, we were big on making practices stimulating, challenging, and interesting; our goal being to entice them, not force them. We also tried to make each athlete feel important to the success of the team as often as possible, by pointing out the various ways the athletes positively impacted the team and by lauding them in front of the team. But we did keep attendance, not only as a way to monitor each athlete's progress, but also as a key measure of how "into it" the whole team was. We calculated the ratio of attendees at practice to the number of team members available (i.e. in town). For example, if our team had 100 swimmers, with 10 out of town (on vacation, at camps, etc.), if 75–80 showed up for practice on an average afternoon, it was an indication that we were doing a pretty good job of motivating our athletes to want to be there.

7. "Want To"Motivation: Doing It For Oneself

These athletes have developed a burning passion to improve and succeed, and have consciously dedicated themselves to the sport. In other words, they have arrived at the pinnacle of the motivational ladder—self-motivation. Again, this internal fire is generally not fueled purely by a love for the sport, but rather by a combination of factors, including the following:

- A desire to achieve personal goals, such as a personal best effort or placing.

- Pride in the athlete's school, club, or community.

- An inner will to succeed (this sport just happens to be the medium).

- Inspiration from coaches, friends, parents, and others who believe in the athlete, or from events that influenced the athlete.

- A love for this particular sport and all its intricacies (for instance, for a swimmer; the smell of chlorine, the feel of the water as one slices through it, the uniqueness of being an individual sport yet so strongly team oriented as well, the rhythm of the practice clock and how one's brain and actions are so tied to it, etc.).

These are just some of the factors that combined, create and reinforce self-motivation. The lessons that coaches and others teach to self-motivated athletes tend to be more fully received, taken to heart, and applied to other areas of their lives than with any other motivational type. *One of our ultimate objectives should be to help our athletes ascend to as high a motivational level as possible*, and for as many as possible to become self-motivated.

Please keep in mind that though many pre-adolescent children often instantly fall in love with a certain sport or sports, few *know* this is the activity they want to commit to for years to come. Those conscious decisions usually come sometime during early adolescence or even later. However, by making the sport fun and membership on the team desirable, by focusing on the athlete's improvement instead of rank, and by taking a personal interest in every one of your team's athletes, a coach can help create extremely positively and intensely motivated children. Certainly they will be more inclined to continue with and even fully embrace the sport as they advance in age.

Motives and Techniques

Thus far we have explored different types of motivation and ranked them in order of overall effectiveness and desirability, both short-term and long-term. Now we want to explore what generally stimulates a younger versus an older age group athlete, and examine an array of high-quality techniques a coach can use to build self-motivation..

Major Motives by Age Group

1. Kindergarten (ages 5–6)

Five- and six-year-olds are eager to tackle new tasks and test themselves. Excessive amounts of time standing in line or sitting and waiting go against their natural grain. For them, the *doing* is paramount, while the *result* (winning or losing) engages their attention temporarily, and then is swiftly forgotten. Therefore, plan practices and contests to involve each of your young

---

How Coaches Can Build Self-Motivation in Their Athletes

1. **Make the Sport Fun!** Make your sport as challenging, exciting, fascinating, *fun* as possible. In addition, teach and express a love for your sport, for its unique and wonderful qualities. Turn your charges on to the sport you coach!
2. **Build a Strong C-A Connection.** Get to know your athletes right from the get go. Consistently interact with them, numerous times on a daily basis if possible. *Build* your relationships, don't just maintain them. With strong relationships in place, your athletes will grow to trust you (which builds their confidence in you and the program), putting you in a better position to positively influence them in all ways.
3. **Help Them Improve!** When competence increases in the athlete, increased desire inevitably follows.
4. **Teach, Remind, then Praise Your Athletes as They Learn, Then Embrace the Steps to Success.** Teach them to embrace habits of success, such as intelligent time management, goal setting, and the ethos of hard work and focus: all engines that will drive them toward their goals. Exhort them to embrace the process by putting out great energy toward worthwhile goals so that they are succeeding each and every day.
5. **Help Your Athletes Find That Powerful Driving Motive or Motives.** Why is the athlete knocking him or herself out in this sport? To help the team win a championship? To set records? To be the very best? Often, a combination of powerful motives drives the athlete. All athletes push harder, the stronger the ultimate motives. As you help them set their short- and intermediate-term goals, make sure such goals line up with the athletes' respective long-term objectives.
6. **Use Higher-Rated Motivational Methods.** You are building their motivational level over time. Fear motivation for example, a lower-rated method, actually *reduces* motivation over time. If you take the extra time to use such higher-quality methods as enticing and inspiring your charges, you'll find it will always pay off in the end.

---

athletes in as much activity as possible. Recognize that an excessive number of rules, restrictions, and criticism can cause children of this age to question their efforts and may lead to a pullback in participation.

Giving instruction to children this young can often be a challenge, too. When learning a skill, many children will have difficulty understanding your explanation. As a general rule, the younger the athlete, the more they need to be shown, not merely explained to. Often the use of vivid imagery or storybook or movie examples can help them click right in to what you are trying to get across as well. Remember, these children love games. That's their definition of fun. And they very much enjoy using their imaginations and playing "let's pretend." Therefore, frame skills or lessons as games and play; you'll be speaking their language and using what they love to do to reach them.

2. Elementary School

As they grow older, children's thought processes become more logical, flexible, and organized. (Although one consequence of their growing up is that they tend to tap into their imaginations less, they certainly still use them!) The great thing is that because they are so much more able to understand your instructions, they *take* instruction much more easily and willingly and can concentrate for longer periods of time. Nevertheless, these are still the "play" years, and all they want is action. Sitting still is tantamount to purgatory, and the final result is secondary to the fun of trying and doing. Even though a child of this age is better able to handle criticism, make sure it is constructive, and that doses of praise and encouragement are dished out in plentiful portions.

The "Compliment Sandwich" is an especially wonderful motivating/teaching technique for this age group. To serve the "sandwich," the coach will first praise the athlete. Since we all love praise, we tend to pay closer attention after we get it. Therefore, the young athlete's mind will be open to what the coach has to say next— the (constructive) criticism or suggestion on how to improve. Following the critique, the coach offers more words of encouragement or praise, helping the youngster feel good about himself or herself and eager to work on improving the skill. An example of this technique applied to a young softball player: "Emily! Wow! Are you working hard on your swing today, and it is leveling out just like you want it to. Make sure you keep your eye on the ball the whole way in. Keep concentrating like you have been, and you will start making contact more often!"

In addition to the enjoyment of *action*, pre-adolescent children love to please (the coach) and to show they are growing up. Therefore, ask them to help you when you might need a hand, such as when bringing out or putting away equipment. It blows me away that when we put in the lane lines before a swim practice, there is a line of youngsters, ready and eager to swim them to the other end. They feel important and needed

3. Middle School/Jr. High (ages 10–11 to 13–14)

Major physical changes are starting to happen to this age children and to their peers. Self-consciousness increases while self-esteem may fall. In addition, they will begin to question who they are, what they do well, and where they fit in. Having friends and being accepted by their peer groups now become far more powerful motivating forces than, say, playing games. Keep in mind that in early adolescence children want and need structure (though they may not always act like it). To avoid role confusion, be the undisputed leader and provide that structure in the form of rules and guidelines of behavior, and by offering intelligent, challenging practices.

Children this age are now becoming more concerned with the outcome of contests. Their caring more about their peers translates into caring more about the team and how it performs. Their concept of fun has started to shift as well. Though games and play-for-play's-sake do still motivate to some extent, early adolescents are more ready to take on challenges and work on meeting goals than before.

4. High School (ages 14–15 to 17–18)

Peers and social comfort are the prime motivating forces at this age. And if they weren't before, boys are now thoroughly into girls, and vice-versa. With regard to athletics, the desire to win and to do what it takes to get there have become of major importance. As a result, striving toward the accomplishment of goals is tremendously satisfying and worthwhile. Games-for-games-sake has retreated as a prime motivating force (though high school athletes do love fun challenges, and still enjoy an occasional game). In fact, coaches often find that at this age dedicated athletes will actually become angry at times if you play too many games, goof around too much, or otherwise distract them from what they are trying to accomplish.

Techniques for Building Motivation in Your Athletes

What follows are general suggestions on how to motivate your athletes. These techniques work with any age and will help build interest in the sport, improve your C-A connection with each athlete, and raise their confidence in themselves and in their capabilities:

1. Hook 'em!

The beginning of any season finds some athletes at their most vulnerable. They may be new to the team and their teammates, uncertain about their skills, or at a loss as to where they fit in. Especially during those first few practices, get to know everyone's name and show an active interest in each athlete. *Show them you care*, and do it right away. Many a fence sitter will come on board, and everyone will tend to get out of the gate more fired up.

2. Take a Personal Interest in Each Athlete

Do this not just in the beginning of the season, but always. Show your athletes you care, genuinely, about them as people, not just as athletes. In fact, show each that you think he and she is *valuable and special*. By treating your athletes in such a way, the cancer of favoritism will not have a chance to take hold. Because all are special, none will appear to be *the* favorite. Also, by your caring so much for them, they will tend to care more about you and the team. You won't need to demand it. It will just happen.

Note: There are some who believe that coaches should focus mainly on athletes who are serious and committed, that those athletes deserve your attention more given that there's only so much attention to go around. Moreover, by shunning those who are not as motivated, coaches will (so the argument goes) cause the less motivated to want more of the coach's attention and therefore to work harder to get it. However, coaches who primarily work with athletes in middle school, or younger) deal primarily with athletes who are too young to know what they want yet. At this age, many are just testing your sport as one of many possible activities; others are in fact unmotivated "have to" types that still are malleable and open to inspiration by the right approach. *Your job is to try to increase their motivation level, not give up on them!* Remember, the younger age group athletes will view your shunning them as "he doesn't like me or care about me" instead of "I should work harder," and you will lose many who could have developed a love for your sport as a result.

3. Make It Fun for Them

Know how your age group defines fun, then make sure they get it! We have already defined a few activities that are the most fun and the most motivational for each age group. However, don't be afraid to try new things and build in lots of variety. "New," "interesting," and "variety" are all ingredients that go into making your sports program fun.

4. Look For and Create Competitive Opportunities to Succeed

This dictum applies more to your less-skilled athletes, but applies at times to all. With regard to competitions, try as much as possible to put your athletes, no matter what their ability level, in situations where they are truly *competitive*, where they have a fighting chance. The United States Swimming organization (U.S.S.—the sport's national governing body) has a meet format that accommodates this aim by seeding each swimmer according to time. Thus, a swimmer whose best time is 38 seconds will race with competitors whose best times are 37, 38, or 39 seconds. Not 32 seconds. Result—automatically tight competitions, and all who are in a race have a real chance to win. In sports where ability level isn't as cut-and-

---

The Effect of Taking a Personal Interest in the Athletes

One summer a few years ago I was asked to help coach the Illinois State Zone Team, an all-star team of the best swimmers in the state. I didn't know 95 percent of the swimmers I would be coaching, so I memorized the fifty or so names of the athletes I would be responsible for. Then I learned each of their top events and their best times in those events.

To what use did I put this information? During the first warm-up session, before each pushed off, I asked my athletes to tell me their names. Upon hearing their name, I'd tell *them* their club team name, their best event or two, and their best event times. It blew them away. Immediate C-A connection. ("This guy knows my times!" He actually knows *me*!"). They saw I cared enough to learn something about them and that I was there to help them do well. Needless to say, I was able to do my job a lot better and have more fun in the process, and so did they.

---

dried, it can be more of a challenge for coaches to match up their athletes with others of comparable skill, yet there are still innumerable opportunities. Bottom line—coaches need to be aware that mere participation doesn't necessarily equate to success (imagine a bench-warmer being inserted into the line-up to satisfy Little League participation requirements, then being blown away by an all-star pitcher's fast-fast ball!)In practice as well as in contests, we need to do our best to create situations that promote a realistic chance for success.

In addition to your creating situations that help them succeed, teach your athletes *how* to compete. Not just the intricacies of their specific sport or position (race strategy, moves, etc.), but also how to become mentally (visualization and other confidence and awareness-building methods) as well as physically (proper sleep, stretching, etc.) prepared to compete successfully. Finally, help your charges (especially the newer and/or younger ones) understand and internalize the link between hard work and improvement; that they have the power to create their own longer-term success through their own efforts.

Note: You are not coddling your athletes when you give them a fighting chance, just leveling the playing field when possible and appropriate, so your athletes can experience tight competition as often as possible. That said, part of our job also must be to help our athletes learn to deal with failure. In terms of life skills, handling failure graciously and positively, with the attitude of "what have I learned from this loss or these mistakes?" is just as important as succeeding. Teaching how to handle failure is critical to helping these young athletes grow up.

5. Discover Other Major Motivations Your Athletes May Have

What reasons, other than the usual ones such as improvement, friends, and fun, do your athletes have for participating? On the positive side, how many of your athletes really want to be the very best? Certainly we coaches try to instill that fire in all our athletes, but do you really know who has that extreme desire? It's a coach's job to find out (via observation, questionnaire, or one-on-one meeting, for instance) and make sure those athletes are being adequately challenged.

At the other extreme, how many of your athletes are with your program not because they want to, but because they have to? As previously noted, you'll usually have a number of children who begin the season basically unmotivated. For this type of child, developing desire in them is the very best use of your energy. Develop their motivation to succeed and they will start paying attention, trying harder, and improving faster. I call it the "Sponge Effect," because once properly motivated, athletes suck up knowledge and instruction like a sponge soaks up water. Identify unmotivated participants and focus much of your energy toward building their appreciation and enjoyment of your sport.

Realize that there are myriad motives for athletes joining your program—participating because it's a great way to get noticed by the other sex, or because best buddy Johnny signed up, or because an athlete wants to use your sport to get in shape for another (swimming for water polo, or cross country for track, for instance). Find out, one way or another, what is driving your athletes. You will certainly have a better chance of pushing the right buttons if you do.

6. Praise—The Art of the Compliment

I have never met a person who didn't appreciate a heartfelt, genuine compliment. The recipient feels appreciative and responds positively because she did something well, and it was noticed. It also showed that you, the coach, are not only aware, but also care enough to point it out. But *praise is mere flattery if done to curry favor, and meaningless if false.* Therefore, when praising, keep the following in mind:

- Be truthful. Our job is to guide athletes, to point them in the right direction, and to help them get to their destination. We can't do that if we give them false information. Therefore, don't say "well done!" if it isn't.

- Broaden your awareness of all the athlete is doing, and therefore what is praiseworthy. That knowledge will yield more areas for potential compliments. Effort, technique, discipline, and sacrifice, are wonderful qualities worth praising. In addition, athletes who are supportive and encouraging of their teammates should be recognized.

- Praise the performance and improvement more than the outcome. In many sports, such as many track and field events, bowling, and swimming, the athlete has zero control over what his competitor does anyway. Yet even with direct competition sports, like basketball or football, focus on what your athletes can control, and make it a point to let them know when they are doing their job well.

- Praise effort (what they do and try to do), not inherent talent (capabilities and attributes they were born with). Praising effort emphasizes a variable the child is in control of, an area he or she can do something about. Complimenting things like inherent intelligence, beauty, or size do nothing for the child because they just *are*, and therefore can't be changed or improved upon. If anything, complimenting talent over effort often leads to increased pressure ("I was praised, so coach expects more of me") without an escape valve ("What do I do to improve if I can't change what just *is*?").

- Do not let the outcome dictate whether you compliment your athletes! One common fault coaches have is the fear that if they praise an individual or the team after losing, the team will lose motivation to win, in other words, that the coach is sending a counter message in support of losing. Hokum! All your athletes should be told when they improve, just as they should know when they are doing something incorrectly.

- Unless you have a really good reason to do so, do not withhold praise when it is deserved. Some coaches choose to withhold compliments, thinking it might make the athlete too soft, or that it will water down their motivational message later on. Granted, we all have our own ways of motivating. But simply put, withholding deserved praise is just a missed opportunity, both for guiding your athletes and for inspiring them.

How often one uses praise will vary with personality, style, and age (younger age groupers generally need and respond favorably to praising more often, but truthful praise goes down well no matter what the age). Some coaches feel that complimenting too often waters down the impact of the compliment, and to a certain extent, they have a point. To be sure, one shouldn't shower one's athletes with praise just because it is supposed to help motivate them. But if sincere, and timed and delivered well, praise is one of the most powerful and positive of motivators.

7. Convince Your Athletes of the Importance of What They are Doing

This may sound too obvious. Yet whether they are involved in an individual match, race, meet, game, or whole season, make sure your athletes understand *what* is important and *why*, including why each of your athletes matters to the team. We often overlook this point, assuming our athletes know not only what's at stake, but why their performance is so crucial to the team's success. This is especially valuable for older age groupers. Conversely, for many younger athletes, those who don't care as much about the outcome or who have trouble with winning and losing, conveying such a message will either fall on deaf ears, or create too much pressure, thus producing the opposite effect of what you intended. Therefore, as a general rule, only use this motivational "tool" when age and commitment levels warrant.

8. Teaching the Importance of Goal Setting

When traveling to a far away destination, we typically need directions (maps, signs, etc.) so as not to drive around aimlessly, wasting time and energy. Like travelers, athletes are guided in the direction of their energies by the setting of short-, intermediate-, and long-term goals. We will discuss goal setting at length in the next section.

9. Keep Finding New Challenges

The first step for athletes who are old or savvy enough to understand what goals are about should be to set *and commit to* certain goals for themselves. The next step, of course, is to help them achieve those goals, by teaching, training, and motivating. To that end, make sure your athletes are continually challenged in practice. Devise new, different, more advanced, or just plain harder challenges. Try not to allow your group to get to a certain level and then just sit there–plateau. Stimulate them in various ways to keep shooting for the stars, and they will at the very least keep improving in some manner.

10. Creating Respect Between Coach and Athlete

Building and maintaining a strong, positive coach-athlete relationship based on each other's trust and respect creates a consistent, powerful, and

---

A Most Amazing Motivational Technique

This move works every time—by praising someone who's just performed, those next in line will want to do better. Here's the setting: It's swim practice and we're practicing 25-yard swims; I want the athletes to use their best technique possible, and some are still pushing off with poor form. The first wave (first person in each lane) pushes off. Immediately, I see that the Lane 5 swimmer has a great streamline (tight arrow-looking body position). Before I launch the second wave, I'll yell out, "Did you see Hannah"s streamline! Wow! Unbelievably tight!" (Of course they didn't see Hannah; they're getting themselves ready for their turn. It's the power of suggestion that has such an impact.) Off goes the second wave. It is simply astounding how well the second wave of swimmers perform! Everyone has an amazing streamline. In the few seconds before the third wave starts, I'll say something like' "Unbelievable! No way anyone can do a better streamline as a group than the second wave! It just can't be done!" Guess how well wave number three does?

There's a whole lot going on here, including some great motivational forces. (1) The athlete's pride is on the line—they want to do better than their teammates. (2) The coach is obviously watching; the athlete wants to impress. (3) Though the coach is praising someone who can't hear it, the athletes next in line suspect that they will be praised in front of their teammates if they perform well. (4) The practice environment is quite fun and positive. Result: a huge step-up in the quality of the performance. This particular method tends to have a greater impact with younger athletes, but done in a subtler, age-appropriate way, it can work with older, high school athletes as well.

---

long-lasting positive motivational force in an athlete. More than liking a coach, respecting and trusting a coach (and vice versa), makes *all* things go better, some substantially so. Respect is something coaches of younger athletes should model always, and talk about or allude to at least occasionally.

Goal Setting

By itself, the mind is an amazing creation. But it can be so much more. An organized, harnessed, *directed* mind can take the body to unbelievable heights. The key is the degree of focus, and focus increases significantly when one sets goals. For young athletes, coaches need to provide most of the guidance by setting objectives and communicating them to the team. By the time they enter middle school, however, most athletes have become capable of setting personal goals (though coaching-led team goal setting does not diminish in importance).

The following breakdown, by age level, describes athletes' goal setting capabilities and the role coaches play in helping them.

1. Kindergarten (ages 5–6)

Kindergartners typically are unable to focus for long periods; they also are either unaware or care too little about the big picture to want to set objectives. Therefore, any direction must come from you. Since athletics at this age should be primarily about participation and learning, and the focus on improvement over final results, traditional goal setting is of less value anyway. Your occasional guidance as to team objectives should suffice, and any individual goals ought to be confined to the very short term, such as practice objectives ("Let's all do 5 laps") or simple betterment objectives, such as helping swimmers learn a new stroke.

2. Elementary School (ages 6–7 to 10–11)

These young athletes are starting to get a sense that focused, sustained effort yields continued improvement. Yet very few have developed the ability to gauge specifically what are challenging, yet realistic individual goals. So question them. Point out some reasonable objectives to shoot for. As far as written goal-setting goes, expose them to the very basics. For example, have them finish sentences you craft, such as "I want to improve my_____ skills," or use multiple-choice questions to help them decide and commit to basic, understandable objectives. Even as you teach them, don't expect your young athletes to pick up on, or put much energy into, the concept right away. Most of them will not fully understand their own capabilities and improvement trajectory well enough to set intelligent performance goals or to care enough to want to work toward such specific objectives. Point them toward simpler goals, such as effort and attendance objectives, as an easier way to introduce the concept. Also, recognize that there are always a few who are either already extremely committed to the sport or who will grasp the concept at an earlier age.

An example: I once had an eight-year-old who was extraordinarily tuned in to the goals he set, and who did as good a job as most teenagers of re-setting and re-focusing once he achieved shorter-term goals. His season of improvement was amazing, principally because he was so locked in to the whole goal setting and re-setting process. Because of exceptions like this young man, and because most older elementary school age children at least understand the concept to a degree, this is a good time to expose them to the process.

Team goals, too, grow in importance as youngsters move into the later years of this stage, so definitely discuss and promote team objectives often, keeping your athletes collectively united and committed.

3. Middle School (ages 10–11 to 13–14)

If your athletes haven't been exposed to individual goal setting yet, teach them now. They should be able to understand the process and be enough in tune with their capabilities to set meaningful objectives. Be sure to teach them the difference between, and importance of, short-term and long-term goals, and drive home the importance of re-setting one's objectives so that they always have a target to shoot for. Most will embrace the process once they experience it.

From a team goal perspective, since results are becoming more and more important, talk up your team goals. In addition, remind your athletes that each of them is of unique and special value to the team.

4. High School (ages 14–15 to 17–s18)

For this age, the fun has almost entirely become about taking the challenge, working toward a goal, and enjoying the satisfaction from achieving an objective. What's more, high school athletes are fully capable of intelligent goal setting, and gain so much by doing so. Therefore, make goal setting an integral part of your program. In addition, if you have access to your athletes during pre-season, a great idea would be to have them think about, then write down, what it is they want to get out of the season, including their aspirations for the team and for themselves.

With respect to team goals, a discussion with team members (as opposed to imposing your opinion only) about what the team is shooting for is the best route to follow. Simply put, if the team members feel they have a hand in deciding their objectives (their fate, if you will), they will buy more fully into those objectives. You, the coach, will of course inform and guide their thinking. But, critically, they will feel invested in the process and in the decision. The more it can be a *team agreed decision*, the more each team member will be motivated to do his or her part.

Teaching Individual Goal Setting and Achieving

The basics of goal setting and achieving appear obvious: choose a goal, then strive toward, and ultimately realize, that objective. Well, yes, goal setting is not rocket science. However, if an athlete (or anybody) wants to be consistently successful with self-motivation, it helps to understand the inner workings of successful goal setting. The following are guidelines aimed at ensuring the athlete's success with this most powerful of self-motivators.

Remember, intelligent goal setting is not an end in itself. The athlete is *defining* the desired objective, which helps motivate the athlete toward *achieving* a result. The two—pinpointing an objective, then reaching it— are inextricably linked.

- Create objectives that are challenging, so the athlete has to work for them.

- Set goals that are *realistic.* They need to be attainable in the mind of the athlete, so that he or she truly believes, and therefore puts out the effort necessary to reach them. For goals to be realistic, athletes need be honest with themselves about their capabilities. Ultimately, best results are achieved when the athlete sets goals that are both challenging *and* realistic.

- For best results, athletes should set their own goals, as opposed to the coach or others deciding for them. Now it's true that for the best possible working relationship between coach and athlete to flourish, the coach should know what the athlete's objectives are. In the case of younger athletes, or ones new to the goal-setting process, the coach should offer advice on which aims are appropriate. But, in the end, for those goals to mean the most, the athlete is the one who should ultimately decide them.

- Goals should be as *specific, clear, and vivid* as possible. Put another way, the more general or hazier an objective, the less of a grip it will have on the athlete's imagination and desires. There are two ways to go about this. One, make the goal itself simple, clear, obvious— to achieve 100 takedowns in a season (wrestling); to break a minute in the 100-meter freestyle (swimming); to exceed 60 feet in the shot put or run a sub-four-minute mile (track and field); to run five miles a day (training for most any sport). All are simple round numbers that are easy to remember. Two, keep the goal front and center in the athlete's mind by displaying it in prominent places so that the athlete is constantly reminded of the objective. For instance, create aphorisms or make posters that can be displayed on a bedroom wall or bathroom door. Or suggest the athlete keep a log with the goals prominently displayed. All are ways to remind the athlete of what all his or her efforts are going toward.

- Goals should be as *measurable* as possible, so athletes can keep track of their progress. For sports such as track, cross-country, skiing, bobsledding, biking, and swimming, the clock does the measuring. Distance and height are calibrated for the field events in track and field. Averages such as on base percentage or slugging average for baseball, or yards-per-carry for a football running back help tell the tale in these sports. Some other sport-specific goals that can be easily measured include rebounds (basketball), pins and takedowns (wrestling), goals (soccer, hockey, water polo), and touchdowns (football). Even many of the so-called subjective sports have aspects to them that can be measured, such as revolutions in the air while performing certain figure skating maneuvers. And, of course, for all sports there are the many attendance, practice, and fitness goals one can set, such as the number of practices attended each week, number of times bench pressing a certain weight, or the time it takes to run a set of arena stairs.

- To stamp a goal more firmly in the athlete's memory bank, and to help commit more fully to the goal, write it down. As the early sports psychologists used to say, "*Ink it, don't just think it*"!

- Perhaps, most critically, teach how to *create and re-set* short-, middle-, and long-term goals. Using a typical sports season as a frame of reference, a short-term goal would be one that is attainable within a few days or weeks, the long-term goals would be those the athlete wants to accomplish by season's end, and any mid-range goals would be created to bridge that gap. However, short-term goals can include what the athlete wants to accomplish that day, and long-range goals can certainly include lifetime objectives, such as a young biker's quest to eventually win the Tour de France. Therefore, the time frame that denotes short-, mid-, and long-term goals is unique to each athlete with regard to what he or she wants to accomplish, and how quickly. The real key to goal setting is to recognize that it is an ongoing process: Once a goal has been reached, re-set it! Progress then tends to continue unbroken. Moreover, no goal is too easy when goal *setting*, since one that is attained "too quickly" is merely re-set. One other vital point—achieving *any* goals, including short-term goals, is not only fun and satisfying in its own right, but will also provide motivational fuel for the continuing quest to accomplish the longer-term goals on which the athlete has set his or her sights.

- For best success at improvement measuring and goal achieving, *set goals in areas you have control over*. For instance, it's better for a basketball player to set a rebounds-per-game goal than to have an objective of winning the rebounding title, because she or he has no control over what the other players in the league accomplish. This does not mean athletes shouldn't have placement goals at all. Quite the contrary. We all want to win, or get third instead of seventh. However, those types of objectives don't measure *progress* as clearly or objectively as those the athlete has control over, and winning will be attained *as a result of* the athlete's efforts to realize the personal goals she has more control over.

• As your athletes become more capable at setting and achieving goals, encourage them to think bigger. Challenge them to reach above and beyond. The amazing achievers have been those who greatly expanded their definition of what was realistic and what was possible.

Creating and Achieving Team Goals

The process of setting and achieving team goals takes athletes beyond their own private world to a higher place where the accomplishment of group objectives often occurs by sacrificing individual desires and glory for the greater good of the team. What tremendous value for young athletes to discover how to work together and push, cheer, and otherwise support each other toward realizing the team's objectives. When a team willingly puts the goals of the team first, and strives and sacrifices in a united effort to accomplish those objectives, its members often accomplish more than conventional wisdom would have believed. *Synergistic* is the word used to describe the state of those teams who accomplish more as a unit than they ought to have been capable of doing as a collection of individuals. Perhaps the best example in this country may be the United States' 1980 Olympic hockey team's winning of the gold medal against astronomical odds. The players were mere amateurs going up against professionals from the U.S.S.R. as well as superior players from a number of other countries. Yet they played as one and never stopped believing they could come out on top.

Though results like the "miracle on ice" don't happen very often, creating a synergy that results in accomplishment above and beyond what was thought possible is a worthy goal for any coach. The beginning of that process is the intelligent setting of team goals. Here are a few guidelines:

When coaching athletes up to and including middle school, keep in mind that—

- Team goal-setting for five-to-seven-year-olds isn't necessary or even desirable. Keep them focused on skill improvement and fun.

- Athletes from mid-elementary school age up through middle school increasingly are motivated by the desire to best the other team. However, you as coach are usually the only one who knows enough about your team's (and your opponent's) capabilities, so you should be the one to set intelligent team objectives.

- Periodically remind your athletes of their objectives and how the team is doing.

- To further drive home teamwork, recount examples of athletes' sacrifices, accomplishments, and efforts that helped the team. In addition, recount tales of how other teams meshed and sacrificed, resulting in great victories and stupendous accomplishments. Make it desirable, make it *in*, to have sacrificed for the greater good of the team.

- Doing all of this will create an environment that promotes team first. Nevertheless, when dealing with younger children, realize that your athletes will be motivated by your efforts at team goal-setting only up to a point. Because results, and the whole process of striving to achieve the best results, are not as important to them, they will generally care less than older athletes. Be happy with what you do accomplish, and know that what is of greater value is the groundwork you have laid that will bear richer fruit the older they get.

When coaching high school athletes—

- Listen to your captains, have team discussions, and give your athletes a hand in the goal-creation process. As a result, they will more strongly support and work toward the realization of those goals.

- Periodically remind the team of what you collectively are shooting for, and further motivate them by giving them updates on how your team is progressing vis-à-vis the competition.

- Promote teamwork and teambuilding. Make a big deal about team members who performed acts that aided the team to the detriment of their own glory, and constantly promote the concept of sacrificing for the greater good. Tell stories about how other great teams worked together to surmount huge odds and accomplish amazing things.

Finally, when coaching any age group:

- Be challenging yet realistic in your goal setting and advising. Know your squad's level of competence, and don't push and harangue your athletes toward goals that are unreachable. If the team has a shot, go for it! Otherwise, do not set them up for failure.

- Be creative. Goal setting is easier when your team is competitive; in other words, if your team is comparable to most of the competition you will face. With such a team, you are in the hunt for some kind of trophy or lofty position, and team pride is usually high. Your goals tend to be easier to create and (for the athletes) to buy into.

    —But how about coaching a team that is a perennial cellar dweller? What can you do, in the form of team goals, to motivate such a group? Since championships and trophies are a fantasy, at least in this situation, set improvement goals of all types. For instance, if your team hasn't won a game in three years, winning one game, any game, is an obvious focus. Or, in some sports, make a big deal of holding the opposition to as few points as possible. For sports where there is a league championship meet, such as in track and field or swimming, set goals relating to point totals. As an example, there might be ten teams in the league, and you may traditionally finish in the bottom third, but can you score more points than you did in the previous season?

Will any of these goals prove motivational? Absolutely, if they are challenging, yet reachable, and you talk them up and make a big deal of their importance. Be assured, you are not accepting mediocrity when you set goals such as those in the examples above. To climb a ladder, you have to advance one rung at a time. Intelligent goals not only motivate, but result in improvement as well. Furthermore, team expectations, and consequently objectives, will automatically be higher the following season because your team became better by embracing, then accomplishing, *this* season's objectives. Momentum toward more far-reaching objectives will build. Hey, why *can't* your team go from last to first eventually!

"Burnout" and the Unmotivatable Child

Every so often you will have a child on your team who, despite your best efforts, remains unmotivated, or regresses in desire. If the team you coach has a short season, or has only a few weeks left in it's season, and the child's commitment and participation are minor, continue to motivate the best you can and play out the string, making sure, of course, that the unmotivated one or ones aren't disrupting the activity for others. Maybe it's the activity, maybe it's you the child doesn't like, and maybe it involves reasons beyond easy understanding. In severe cases make the parents aware that Tommy or Sara is showing major signs of disliking the activity and suggest that maybe there is something else out there that will suit their child's fancy in the future.

If the athlete has been in the sport a long time, if the sport is ongoing (not seasonal), or if you have coached that child long enough to know him or her more thoroughly and you see signs of a regression in motivation, do talk to the parents. Commonly known as *"burnout"*, a loss of motivation or even the development of real antipathy for the sport sometimes occurs. An athlete will go from being either reasonably or even highly motivated to listlessness or even outright rebellion. It could be caused by a broken coach-athlete (CA) connection. Sometimes it's caused by a parent's taking over of the child's sport, so that it's more the child swimming for the parent instead of for himself or herself. The possible reasons for a child's sudden lack of interest are numerous, and a coach usually can't know them all. Early symptoms include increasingly being late for practice, acting out in practice, and pulling back in effort and focus. More severe symptoms include newfound sullenness and unresponsiveness and actions that show a lack of respect. Over time, you may find out something that will help you turn things around, or not. Here, too, it's ultimately the parents' decision, but if you can't figure out how to turn things around and the child is miserable, suggest trying another team (if it seems to be the team that is at issue, not the sport), or another activity if it is the sport the child is having problems with.

Some Concluding Thoughts on Motivation

Instruction, training, motivation—these are the three main ingredients that make up successful coaching and, if done well, guarantee progress. Of the three, one could argue that an athlete's motivational level is the single most critical element in the overall improvement picture. It, more than the other two elements, regulates the speed of an athlete's progress. Perhaps even more important, motivation regulates *the quality of the athletes' experience* in that a highly motivated athlete of any age will have more fun, attain greater satisfaction, and get more out of the experience than one who exhibits less desire to succeed. Yet when we coaches plan our seasons we tend to set fitness and performance targets for the team but omit motivation objectives. In fact, we usually don't even think of raising the team's motivational level as a goal to be consciously thought through, let alone established. But we could.

Say it's the beginning of your season. Your team is composed of thirty athletes. You've gotten to know them and deduced that (roughly) five are predominantly fear motivated, ten fall into the "have to" category, ten are mainly reward motivated, and five are at some level of "want to." Thus your team's average motivation level falls somewhere between the motivations of "have to" and reward. Granted, your estimates are subjective, but why not try setting your own motivational goal for the team? Establish a goal of raising fifty percent of your athletes to a "want to," for instance. Then, consciously set about attaining your objective by planning events and actions that will help raise individual motivational levels. Use team outings, team meetings, goal-setting sessions, and so on. Strive, through application of the many techniques we have discussed, to move each athlete closer to self-motivation. Inspire them! Help create that powerful craving that causes them to put out tremendous effort and become like sponges in their desire to soak up everything about improving in their sport! It seems to me that putting even a modicum of thought, planning, and action into improving the motivation of your athletes would pay outsized dividends relative to the effort required.

▶ **Summary Points** ▶ ▶ ▶

▶ Positive motivation is an essential ingredient in any high-quality youth sports program.

▶ Among the three main ingredients in coaching, motivation most often determines the speed and quality of improvement.

▶ Ideally, whatever motivational methods you use should positively impact the athlete, both short- and long-term. Part of the art of coaching is in discerning which method to use, when, and with what intensity so that the impact will be positive in all ways as often as possible.

▶ Coaches should use methods that create and stoke a burning desire; they should learn which methods build desire, and which ones diminish it.

▶ An athlete's major motivators tend to change as the child grows through developmental stages.

▶ Some of the techniques for building motivation in any athletes include—showing interest in each and every athlete, creating opportunities for succeeding, making participation fun, communicating the importance of the mission and their efforts, constantly finding ways to challenge the athletes, and goal setting.

▶ Team goal-setting and achieving take athletes beyond their own individual desires to focus them on a higher, collective purpose.

▶ Some effective goal-setting methods include creating short-, mid-, and long-term goals; immediately re-setting achieved goals ; making goals as measurable, specific, and vivid as possible; and making goals challenging, yet realistic.

Team, Teamwork, and Team Building

It is a special achievement when an individual, having set demanding goals, focuses on those goals, applies himself or herself vigorously over a period of time, and finally reaches his or her objectives. The resulting feelings include joy and deep satisfaction, as well as increased personal confidence that one can successfully handle future challenges. Now, if you imagines those feelings magnified many times over, you begin to understand the added depth and intensity of emotion when a *group* of individuals unites successfully in a common effort to accomplish something difficult and important. Amazing experiences result when a team believes in itself and strives toward a common goal. Some memorable examples include the 1980 US Olympic hockey team's electrifying gold medal run and the New York Mets 1969 miracle World Series victory. Perhaps your daughter's swim team's improbable move from fifth to second place in the league championships may fall into the same category. In each of these cases, the end result of the united team effort was greater than the sum of the efforts of each individual. When this synergy occurs, the positive feelings are extra special and can last a lifetime.

Age group coaches are blessed each season with the unique opportunity to mold a large number of young individuals into a smoothly working, high-achieving unit. The challenge is to take those disparate minds, bodies, and backgrounds and motivate them to pull together and move in the same direction. The result of this unity will be more individual improvement as well as greater team success. Most important, the *quality* of the overall experience is enhanced when the entire team is united and working together. Practices are more emotionally relaxed and fun, yet more is accomplished in them. Teammates develop greater respect for one another. Friendships form and/or deepen. Discipline problems are rare. Potentially disruptive situations rarely get a chance to develop. The athletes are more highly motivated, are focused on the right things for the right reasons, and *want* to be at practice with their teammates. Consequently, your job as coach becomes far more enjoyable and satisfying.

In essence, a great team experience transforms participation in youth sports from just another activity into something truly special. As you build the team and teach the value of teamwork, you'll be imparting one of the most valuable lessons your young athletes will ever learn: Teamwork means sacrificing for the greater good and working together for the benefit of all (sublimating the "me" for the "we"). As these young athletes grow into adulthood, they will come to realize that the ability to get along and work together with their peers is the foundation of a high-quality life at home, in the community, and in the workplace. After all, the team concept applies to any situation where two or more people are combining their efforts toward a common goal. You, as an age group coach, have the ideal arena for imparting and reinforcing these critical skills. Seize the opportunity!

From Chaos to Synergy: The Evolution of Teamwork as a Skill

The Second College Edition of the *American Heritage Dictionary* defines *chaos* as "a condition or place of total disorder or confusion." Put another way, it's a playground full of youngsters, each doing his or her own thing. Now, if this crowd of energetic youths is going to coalesce into a unit while learning how to play a certain game, then cooperation must occur. In fact, in any sport you'll ever coach, progress requires at least some cooperation. Teamwork is desired, but how much teamwork occurs will be a function of many things, including the athletes' motivation level, their maturity level, and your motivational skills.

Cooperation occurs when people "work or act together toward a common end or purpose." Children are first exposed to cooperation when they begin to play with other children. They begin to realize that at times they must adjust their actions or temporarily suppress their desires. Their ability to cooperate evolves as incidents of shared play occur more often and each child starts to understand why cooperation is important. By the time children join your team, their parents and other significant adults have already impressed upon them the importance of sharing, taking turns, and getting along with others. But there is a world of difference between cooperation ("I understand I must take turns and share") and teamwork ("I *want* to work with my teammates toward this goal we all have"). The difference is in the *degree of willingness* to work together, which is far greater when working toward a common goal. Participation on an age group team presents a wonderful opportunity for young athletes to bridge this gap, to evolve from cooperation to teamwork.

A young child's first age group sports experience is usually his or her first organized team experience. The structure of this training experience (drills, practices, games) intrinsically requires cooperation and creates a framework for teaching and developing teamwork. The age group coach has the perfect opportunity to help a child evolve from cooperation (*passive* acceptance or agreement) to teamwork (*active* initiation of effort involving imagination, ingenuity, and desire). The former evolves into the latter. That is, teamwork is simply cooperation taken to the next level—a child's wanting to help the team and seeking out ways to do so.

A group of athletes progresses from chaos to cooperation, from cooperation to teamwork, and finally to the ultimate level, synergism! *Synergism* is teamwork taken to the *nth* degree. Don Swartz, former director of the Creative Performance Institute (an organization whose main focus was on helping athletes perform better through mental preparation), described it years ago in his "Mental Focus" column (*Swimming World Magazine*, February, 1980):

> Synergism refers to the cooperative action of individuals such that the total effect is greater than the sum of the efforts of each of those individuals . . . .This is (often what is meant) when people . . . say a team has momentum. We have all seen a team that seems to demonstrate magical powers. The evidence of this is a heightened awareness of the total scope of the game or meet coupled with a maximum effort by each individual. The overall effect is that all the breaks go their way and mistakes do not rattle their confidence.

How does this amazing phenomenon come about? Swartz explains:

> Individuals constantly sacrifice themselves and support each other first, themselves second. Everyone is operating in a very positive, dominant climate—which, incidentally, they have created.

Swartz also cites John Brodie, the former San Francisco 49ers All-Star quarterback:,When you have [a team that] knows each other very well and has every ounce of their attention—and intention—focused on a common goal and all their energy flowing in the same direction," then you have created the climate necessary to produce this synergistic effect.

Team Building—What Is It and Why Do It?

The term *team building* describes a coach's conscious or overt actions to build team unity. It primarily involves the teaching and promotion of the value of teamwork, the setting of team purpose and goals, and the systematic building of closer ties within the team. In fact, team building actually starts with the effectiveness of the coach as a leader, as well as with her or his basic attitude toward the athletes.

Why should team building be an important focus of a coach's time, effort, and awareness? First of all, a little effort in this direction has a positive, snowball effect on performance. The more a team's members support each other and work together, the more teamwork occurs and the more production (and of a higher quality) will result. In addition, athletes are exposed to many meaningful social experiences and such life lessons as getting along with one's fellow human beings in a positive team environment. An athlete's richest and most rewarding memories will often stem from this aspect of his or her experience—the team experience. And if those aren't powerful enough reasons to wholeheartedly embrace this aspect of your coaching, consider this: We all naturally desire to belong and be accepted; it's a part of being human. Young athletes want to identify with a group. Therefore it is very important for us as developers of young people to work at helping our athletes feel accepted within the team. As a result they will tend to feel more significant and special. And if you have an eye on increasing your program's size, keep in mind that your age group program's enrollment will grow as more young people find your team to be a haven where they feel as if they truly belong.

A quick word about the amount of teamwork involved in team sports versus individual sports: No matter what sport you coach, teamwork is involved. While it's obvious in such team sports as basketball or soccer, where athletes must constantly interact with one another during the game ,teamwork, or unity of effort, is equally important in individual sports such as track, wrestling, and singles tennis. The difference between them is that the teamwork in individual sports focuses less on the interweaving of skills to create an outcome (a touchdown, for instance), and more on the social and motivational aspects of training with, and supporting each other. In any sport involving more than one person, athletes practice together. This involves disparate personalities coming together to train. Whether they support and assist each other physically and psychologically will determine how much they can achieve, both individually and collectively.

The Most Powerful Team Builder— Coach as Leader

You, as coach, wear many hats—administrator, teacher, strategist, and motivator, to name just a few. Your position automatically confers another role upon you, that of leader, because you initiate all goals, direction, and team organization. Certainly you instigate the improvement of the team and control the quality of your athletes' experiences. To be effective at these tasks and to reach the team's goals require leadership, your leadership. When we talk about *team building*, the conscious, systematic building of team unity, the most effective tool we have as coaches is our power to persuade, to inspire, and to lead. Yet just because one is in a leadership position doesn't mean one is a leader! In fact many coaches lack strong leadership capabilities, and in some cases their programs are mediocre or even fail because of weak leadership. The good news is that these leadership skills can be learned and improved. (We will explore the concept of leadership, as well as touch on some of the main principles involved, later in this chapter.) Certainly any in-depth analysis of what it takes to forge a great team must begin with the role of head coach, for it is he or she who is the prime motivator and catalyst for change and progress.

Team Building Starts with a Coach's Attitude

How tightly knit and united your team becomes will depend largely on the actions you take toward that end. Those particular actions, such as organizing a team outing or praising an athlete in front of his peers, stem from the importance you place on team building. Team-building attitudes have their foundation in your answer to the basic question —how do I feel about my athletes? Your attitude toward them goes a long way in defining not only how they feel about themselves, but also how they feel toward their teammates.

The Foundation Attitudes of Team Building

1. **All are of value.** Young, old, short, tall— all of us have unique talents, capabilities, and ways in which we can contribute to society. Some of us, especially the young, haven't fully discovered what makes us special. Nevertheless, there is that potential for "something special" in all of us. Coaches who recognize this uniqueness will use their athletes far more effectively, resulting in a team that will accomplish more and athletes who'll have a higher quality experience. Each team member will have a role or roles because the coach will seek out each member's strengths and utilize them. (An invaluable by-product of a coach's search for team members' strengths will be the discovery and acknowledgement of their weaknesses and needs, areas the coach and members of the team can attack and improve upon together.)

2. **All are important to success.** This is the obvious corollary to #1. There is simply no doubt in my mind as to the validity of this point. Whether the athlete is a front-line point scorer or a second stringer (to use only one measure of value, point scoring), all team members have something to offer. *Assume* that all team members are important to the success of your team, and therefore worthy of your attention, and you will reap the benefits. Points are not the only measure of value. That view is myopic. You need leaders, empathetic personalities, artists, super-hard practice workers, cut-ups, friends, depth in the lineup in case of injury or illness....The list is endless. In any case, it's up to you as coach and team builder to ensure that everyone understand their importance to the team's success.

3. **All are deserving of respect.** It would seem to follow that if we have value, we are deserving of respect. Therefore, no factor, especially age, should prevent the giving and receiving of respect. Yet, too often we think of young children, adolescents, even high school-aged youth as "less than" and don't grant them the respect they deserve. That is the single biggest mistake a teacher of young people can make, for two reasons. First, treating a child as "beneath respect" reduces the quality of communication between coach and student, reducing the quality of the experience. Second, perhaps because most of society doesn't view children as deserving the same respect as adults, the young's response when they *do* receive it

is immediate, positive, and intense. They try harder and accomplish more, are prouder of themselves, and tend to give that respect back, to their instructors and to others. I do not want to call it a motivational technique, because it isn't a device or method. But keep in mind that the result of treating your athletes like valued individuals will be much like you had performed some amazing motivational feat.

If a coach possesses these Foundation Attitudes, he or she will naturally and inevitably connect more easily and deeply with athletes of any age in much the same way that magnets attract. The coach feels the athlete has value, is important to the coach and the team, and is respected. The athlete feels that vibe, is drawn to the coach's message, and is more willing to give it his or her all.

My attitudes about a person's worth and right to respect crystallized years ago while teaching and coaching at New Trier Township High School. As in most high schools there were many highly motivated, productive students and athletes who attended classes and participated on sports teams at the school. However, there were also young people there who were supposed troublemakers—unmotivated, uncaring, or negative. All types. In reflecting how to handle these young people, I realized that I didn't know them and didn't know what they were like or what they were capable of. So I decided against prejudging and treated them all in the same way—with a certain amount of genuine politeness and respect. Much to my complete amazement, I never had a student or athlete who didn't return that basic respect to some degree and at least put forth some effort. No unreachables. I had unwittingly discovered one of the great secrets of motivation and unity: If you give respect, you will invariably receive it.

The following are just some of the respectful ways coaches can interact with their athletes:

- Instead of always commanding, try asking. • Always be polite.
- Never denigrate the individual, especially in front of the group.
- Give team members important tasks to do.
- Let the athletes make the decisions some of the time and where appropriate.
- Listen to and consider their opinions. Encourage team members to speak freely by responding positively to their heartfelt suggestions.

Don't worry! You're still in control! If respect is not returned, educate your athletes as to what it is and how to behave respectfully toward their coaches, teammates, and anyone else.

We have discussed an athlete's value to the team and why, in the interest of team building, athletes should be given attention and viewed as vital to the team's success. However, also consider that all of your athletes are worthy of attention, focus, and effort because your overall, number-one priority as an age group coach is the development of the individual. In that regard, part of your job should be pointing out to your young athletes some of the areas at which they excel and yet may not see, and what special talents they may possess but do not recognize. By helping them find what they do well and what they can be successful at, you do them a great service. Often, youngsters aren't consciously aware of some of those special qualities with which they were born. Whether those talents apply to the sport you're coaching is immaterial. Truthful observations about qualities the child possesses and may have been totally unaware of can have a tremendous impact, both short- and long-term, on that child's life.

By using the preceding Foundation Attitudes to show athletes their importance in your program, you help make them feel:

- *Accepted.* Socially and psychologically it is huge for a child to feel he or she belongs. And if you, the coach, accept that athlete, so eventually will most of his or her teammates. This is key in the team-building process.

- *Special.* They are special! Give all your athletes attention and point out their good points and at what they can improve upon, and they will feel special. Also, if you view every athlete as important, then the tendency toward favoritism is reduced. The goal, of course, is not to exhibit any overt favoritism—period. Keep in mind that if your athletes feel they're being treated equally, they will unite more readily.

- *Worthwhile.* By periodically pointing out each child's contributions to the overall effort (e.g., "you were key in that relay," or "thanks for demonstrating your backstroke turn to the team"), you're maintaining their awareness that all are vital parts in a smoothly operating, successful group. Too many of them feel that if they aren't scoring points, they have no worth on the team. Although untrue, the opposite is a tough concept to get across. Seize any opportunity to point out other ways in which they contribute (such as being the running leader in practice or the composer of your team's cheers, etc.), and their recognition and appreciation of their own value will increase.

Coach As Role Model

How you act is of enormous importance to your athletes. Whether you like it or not, you're a major role model to them. Yes, they know you have your own unique personality, that humans are all different. Regardless, they spend so much time under your guidance that almost by osmosis you exert a huge influence upon how they think and act, not only by what you say, but also how you say it; not only by what you do, but also by how you do it. How you act is a product of your personality, your beliefs, and your attitudes. Some of those actions, such as explaining that day's practice or working on stroke technique, result from your plans and your overall strategy for achieving the team's goals. Other actions are actually *re*-actions to situations. They emanate from the subconscious and from habit, and reflect your personality and attitude. Examples include how you react to an athlete's performance, or how you choose to field questions during practices. How you behave—what words you use, your overall demeanor, your tone of voice—all tell a person whether you're genuine, positive, or negative, credible, and more.

Your athletes read the signals you send. How you act contributes significantly toward your effectiveness as a coach and will have a bearing on team unity. Loud put-downs and cynical or negative comments or facial expressions tend to result in your athletes having negative feelings about you, themselves, and ultimately the team. Conversely, a smiling face and positive words, actions, and body language will help athletes enjoy being in each other's company. Remember, young athletes view coaches' words and expressions as being of great importance. Be aware of that fact, and you can actually use the role model phenomenon to your benefit. In any event, it is an effective tool, both as a guide for how they should behave, and as a team unifier. Another trick in the bag! Don't underestimate the importance of this phenomenon.

Team Goal Setting

Defining objectives and putting energy and focus toward the achievement of those goals is a blueprint for progress and success. We know that individuals and teams improve at a faster rate when there are goals to sharpen the mind's focus and channel one's energy and emotions more specifically toward a desired result. What may not be understood as well is that the process a coach uses to achieve team goals can act as a tremendous unifying force as well.

Often the single most important team-building activity for a team of older age group athletes (those of upper middle school through high school age) is the setting of major team goals for the season. Whether your main objective is to win the league championship or to defeat the cross-town rival in the big game, specific major challenges around which the whole team can rally are as good an overall team builder as can be found. But how to go about it? For the setting of your team's goals to be successful, two factors must be taken into consideration: the degree to which your athletes take part in the decision making, and how realistic those goals are.

Phil Jackson, in his inspirational book *Sacred Hoops,* notes that "before a vision can become reality, it must be owned by every single member of the group." Perhaps the most effective way to guarantee that your athletes will buy into your team's vision, or goals, is for the members of your team to have input during the decision-making process. If they feel they have a voice and are part of the process, then they will tend to feel more responsible for implementation and realization. Those objectives will become more important precisely because your athletes helped decide on them. They "own" those goals collectively. Hence, they will work harder at seeing that the team achieves what it has set out to do. Remember, shared goal setting can only work if the athletes are experienced and knowledgeable enough to accurately assess their own team's overall capabilities and potential (as well as the capabilities of the opposition, if goals involve team rankings). Otherwise goals may not be realistic.

Adopting unattainable goals can lead to failure, disillusionment, and disappointment. A general rule of thumb is that a team is more able to share in goal setting as the average age of its members increase. As noted before, athletes in primary school have little concept of the big picture, and therefore they cannot realistically envision what their team's objectives should be while older age group athletes can better assess, and get excited about, team goals. So, how should you handle team goal setting, given the range of ages one deals with in age group coaching? If you're coaching high school athletes, have a team meeting early in the season. In addition to giving your assessment of what you as coach believe the team should be shooting for, ask for their opinions. From this discussion a team consensus will form, and the resulting goals will generally be supported by all, because all had an opportunity to contribute to them. If you're coaching younger age groupers, you must decide the team goals and then sell their importance to the team. You must get your younger athletes to take those goals to heart, to commit to them. As Dr. Keith Bell says, "Team building begins with the collective embodiment of a clearly specified team purpose." One way or another, the team must grasp the importance of your team's purpose and goals. If your athletes aren't experienced enough to share in the understanding and defining of those objectives, then you need to get that vision across to them as best you can..

What's an effective way to communicate a vision to young athletes? Paint a verbal picture in clear, easy-to-understand language at your initial team meeting. You might address the team in this way:

> We have finished second to Nottingham in each of the last two years. Our goal is first place. Yes, I know we have never won the Pleasant Prairie Conference since we joined nine years ago, but this year we can do it! Nottingham whipped us two years ago, but we have been working very hard and improving steadily ever since. And if you all remember, they barely beat us last season. If we are consistent with our practice attendance and really push ourselves to the limit, we have a legitimate shot at the League Championship!

You are giving your team background on what has happened and a context in which your objective—the league championship— has some meaning and is believable. You also offer a brief blueprint of how the team can go about accomplishing that objective.

It is again worth noting that during the first few years of an athlete's participation in age group sports, team interests, *per se,* aren't as important as they will be later in their lives. Winning and the team's performance take second place to participation ("I just want to be in there!"). Fun is the magnet that keeps the younger athlete engaged. Let us always keep in mind that the importance placed on winning grows with age, experience, improvement, and increased desire. Eventually, the sport and its outcome become of greater importance to the athlete, as does his or her ability to help select team goals.

Whether you, the coach, are the one selecting team goals or, instead, are guiding the group goal-setting effort, it is vital to have a fair sense of what's a true challenge, yet realistically attainable and ultimately worthy of major commitment and effort. When setting the types of goals that involve ranking your team with other teams in a league or conference, you must be able to accurately assess your team's potential, as well as have a good idea of what the rest of the league or conference is capable of accomplishing. As an example, it's futile to get your athletes excited about moving from second to first in your league if eight Olympians moved into the previous champ's school district in the off-season. Also realize that there are other types of goals than those involving won-lost records and/or rankings. Be creative, and work at tailoring your team goals to your team and league situation.

••

Scenario on Goal Setting: You have just finished your first year as the head coach of your high school swim team. There are six teams in the division, and your team finished last in both the dual-meet and championship standings the previous year. After assessing the strengths and weaknesses of the entire division, you realize that, on the one hand, shooting for first or second place or even winning the majority of your dual meets would be an unrealistic goal for the coming season,. On the other hand, time coupled with heart and effort could quite possibly result in a league championship in the not-to-distant future. But how do you unite and motivate your athletes *now* to put forth the effort needed to reach those (eventual) lofty heights? After all, on the face of it, it appears you have no realistic goals that are headline grabbing and seductive enough to be automatic motivators ("Go for the Gold!" or "Three-peat!"). What to do?

1. **First and foremost, emphasize improvement to your athletes, mainly their own as opposed to rankings vis-à-vis other teams.** Definitely sell them on the long-term goal of a league championship, but then set up numerous short-term goals that are achievable. Success begets success, and as those short-term goals are met, the growing string of successes will give your team more confidence in themselves and in each other (which is a huge uniting factor). For the coming season, realistic ranking-type goals might include moving up to fifth or fourth place in the championship meet, or perhaps winning a dual meet or two. Finishing out of the cellar will initiate a positive, dynamic effect on the team. It will increase confidence, effort, and intensity, which will in turn lead to even more improvement and further success.

2. **Second, make intelligent use of goal setting that is not dependent on how other teams perform.** Make sure your athletes set short- and long-term goals that are based on time, distance, skill improvement, and so on, instead of individual placement or team standings. As a swim coach, for instance, encourage the setting of individual time goals (last year = 23.5, this year's goal is a 22.6) and performance objectives (perfecting the backstroke start) as well as team pride goals such as those involving relays, achieving league or state qualifying cuts, new team records, and so on.

3. **Finally, sell your team on the importance of the goals you have all set.** Make certain they know that these goals are worth great effort. Be sure they recognize that going from sixth to fourth (for your team) is just as important and rewarding as another team's winning the championship. Because it is!

Team-Building Events and Activities

The ultimate result of all your team-building efforts should be a group of athletes that is more united, committed, and smoothly functioning than before. The attitude a coach has toward his or her athletes, the atmosphere created and maintained in practices, the setting of team goals, and the spirit evidenced at events are all integral aspects of this development of a greater sense of *Team*. A group must first get to know one another for respect to develop between teammates and for team pride and unity to blossom. Planned events such as a team potluck dinner or a trip to the water park give your athletes a chance to connect in a more relaxed, enjoyable setting. Teammates get to know one another better and have a good time in the process. A few of these mixers, intelligently spaced throughout the season, will have multiple, positive, long-term ramifications for your team.

Good examples of team building through the intelligent use of planned events occur at many high schools in all sports. The planned team building that existed on the New Trier Township High School swim teams when I first joined the coaching staff was mind-opening for me. A whole raft of activities had been set up at intervals throughout the season. Events ranging from a Freshmen Welcome party early in the season to potluck dinners to activities, such as an apple-picking outing, helped teammates bond and have fun in the process. When athletes joined the swim team, they were gaining a full-fledged, well-rounded social experience—making friends, acquiring a support group, and finding a niche of their own in the social structure of a large school, not merely participating in workouts and meets. First-year swimmers were more apt to return the following year because the team satisfied so many personal needs and desires. Teammates became closer, and friendship and mutual respect, the cement that binds a unit, flourished.

Younger age group teams also thrive on planned team building. Our summer swim team loves to have a day at the water park or an ice cream social after a given practice. And since parental involvement is far more prevalent and necessary with younger children (parents are, in essence, an integral part of your team), parent-child mixers, such as a "kick off" party, allow parents a great opportunity to get to know one another. The fact is, the better teammates know each other, the more unified they will become. There is more than a little truth to the saying, "Those who play together, stay together."

Planned team building works well with any age athlete. However, when considering how much and what kinds of activities, keep this point in mind: As a general rule, the older your athletes are, the more importance they will tend to ascribe to the team and their experience on it. Therefore, figure on planning more team-building activities the older your athletes are. As to the kind of activities, choose age-appropriate activities that involve more social interaction for older athletes—parties, pizza outings, etc. For younger athletes, select more purely play-type activities, like a trip to an amusement park. You definitely don't want to plan a dance with your ten-and-under soccer team!

Pre-season Events and Activities

Many high school sports require some sort of pre-season conditioning period. Coaches should check the rules concerning when (or whether) they can have face time with their athletes before the actual season begins. But whether or not coaches are allowed to be involved directly or not, team pre-season sessions can have a major impact on the season, both from a training and team-building perspective. I have seen many a high school team come together and perform far beyond expectations, only to find out later that the catalyst was their pre-season team-building experience. And it stands to reason: The sooner your team unites, the longer it can perform synergistically and the more the athletes will accomplish.

Though younger athletes generally don't have this type of pre-season conditioning session, coaches can choose any number of actions or activities to start the team-building process before the season begins. You might send a letter to the athletes or speak to them individually (if, for instance, you teach in their school) as a way of letting them know you're interested in them and can't wait to start the season. Another possibility is to have a pre-season kick-off party or other mixer. These are excellent, especially for teams with rapid or total turnover, as a vehicle for helping the athletes and their parents get to know one another. For teams that return all or most of their athletes year after year (such as our summer swim team), you can plan a pre-season reunion. At these boisterous get-togethers, children and parents who may not have seen each other for many months reunite. And though much of the conversation and fun has little to do with swimming, these mixers help the team get jazzed up for the coming season. All these actions and activities, and many others, can help bond young and older youth teams alike.

Pre- and inter-season planned team building actions and activities (other than the pre-season conditioning sessions noted previously) are a part of the coaching job where the athletes' fun and enjoyment at being together are the only requisites. It also gives a coach the chance to spice up the training grind with a little variety. If planned intelligently and carried out well, the result will inevitably be a more unified and happier team. The result is well worth the extra effort.

Every Athlete is of Value to the Team

As previously noted, each athlete brings a unique blend of physical and mental capabilities and personality characteristics to a team. All have something (usually many things) to contribute. But are you as coach aware of those contributions? Are all your athletes, especially the non-point scorers, truly appreciated as important team members by you and the team? More important, is that appreciation being *shown*? To be truly unified, team members need to have pride and respect, for themselves and for each other. Pride in one's own worth is developed as the athlete contributes more to the team, and as he or she is recognized for having contributed. Recognition for a young athlete is the validation that he or she indeed is a key member of the team.

Recognition of an athlete's contributions comes in many forms. By recognition I don't necessarily mean major radio broadcasts or interviews with *Time* magazine. Recognition most often will come with a teammate's "Way to go!" or a coach's pat on the back. Unfortunately, far too many contributions go unnoticed, and athletes' desires can gradually diminish as their contributions are (usually unintentionally) ignored. By learning to spot and appreciate all the ways athletes contribute, a coach gets more out of his athletes and develops greater team unity and pride. What follows is a discussion of the many ways an athlete is of value to his team. My goal here is to shed some light on the more complex picture of all that it takes to bring about great synergistic, team success. In the process I hope to shift the focus from only-the-point-scorer-as-important to a deeper appreciation of how each and every athlete, in his or her own way, adds significantly to any team.

Almost any action or effort, if directed toward helping the team, has value, not only in reaching team goals, but also in acting as a unifying force. Looking at it another way, I can think of only two ways a teammate, any teammate, can detract from a group's positive flow: Either the athlete has such a negative attitude that his or her behavior tends to detract from the team's positive flow or the athlete's focus is directed elsewhere. (Of course, one of the most challenging and ultimately satisfying aspects of coaching transpires when you work with, and eventually help transform, a negative team member into a more positive, confident, committed athlete, or when you can help direct the unfocused child toward improving his skills and aiding the team.)The following are just some of the many positive ways an athlete can benefit the team.

1. *Physical and Mental Effort and Willpower*

Physical and mental effort means athletes giving their all in contests, pushing themselves in practices, and showing up regularly for practice. Any time someone puts out extra effort, the rest of the team is spurred on. The out-of-nowhere maniacal swim on a key relay leg comes to mind as a great motivator for an entire swim team. What a great example and super energy lift! Or how about the hard-as-nails practice swimmer, the girl who hammers every swim and can summon unseen reserves to blast one more set at the end of practice when everybody else is dying. Her teammates derive inspiration from such gutsy performances, and they will tend to be swept up in the challenge. Their pride is on the line, and "If she can do it, I can at least try" is the reaction of a proud, united team to such an effort. Moreover, because we all know that meet performances are ultimately dictated by what you do in practice, the tough practice swimmer is a highly valued commodity on any swim team.

There are several reasons why I have included practice attendance in this section. First, it can be an effort sometimes just to commit to going to practice. For instance, a young swimmer who is not yet fully committed may have second thoughts about showing up on a cold day when the pool heater is broken. Yet that athlete cannot begin to improve until he or she actually gets his or her body to the practice site. Second, an important phenomenon occurs at practices and meets: When you have someone with whom to compete, anyone, you tend to go faster and try harder. Just showing up for practice is *so* important, not just for one's own improvement, but because another athlete is there, sharing the difficulties and triumphs, one with whom a teammate can practice and compete.

2. Positive Reinforcement

Anytime a person has a nice word for another person, it is a positive. When a team member encourages a fellow teammate, good feelings flow, and team unity, as well as performance, improves. And genuine appreciation? It is one of the foundation tenets in Dale Carnegie's groundbreaking study on what motivates people, *How to Win Friends and Influence People.* In it he cites Charles Schwab—in 1921 the first president of U.S. Steel at age 38—as one of the best examples of a man who was not brilliant or the most knowledgeable at his craft, but rather who achieved success through his ability to deal with people.

When revealing his philosophy, Schwab once said, "There is nothing else that so kills the ambitions of a person as criticisms," and, "If I like anything, I am hearty in my approbation and lavish in my praise." Carnegie also notes the difference between flattery (insincere praise) and appreciation (genuine, honest praise). Coaches and athletes alike should be aware that sincere compliments are among the best kinds of reinforcement someone can receive. Situations are omnipresent in which athletes can use positive reinforcement to give teammates a lift. Cheering at contests, offering words of encouragement during practices, and complimenting teammates sincerely at any time are all effective ways to use positive reinforcement. One of my former swimmers put it so well when she noted that "There have been so many 'impossible' sets that became possible for me only because, each time I stopped, someone told me to hang in there or that I was doing fine. Thoughts of giving up *either didn't have the opportunity to surface, or were canceled out* when I heard even a couple encouraging words." Also keep in mind that positive reinforcement between teammates is especially powerful when an older athlete compliments or encourages a younger one.

3. Positive Personality Characteristics

Any person with well-developed "people skills" will be a huge plus for any team, regardless of his or her physical capabilities. They are the "unifiers," the cement that binds a team socially and psychologically. Some "people skills" categories that should be easy to spot on your team include the following:

- *Leadership*—The take-charge mentality. Good leaders, such as many team captains, rally the squad emotionally during close competitions or buck them up during rough practices. They keep an eye out for their fellow teammates and lead by example as well as speech. Good leaders will constantly attempt to help move the team in a positive direction.

- *Enthusiasm*—Enthusiastic people have a passion for life, their sport, and the team. Enthusiasm is a tremendously powerful and positive emotion; it is contagious!

- *Empathy*—People with this quality are able to feel and understand what their friends and teammates are going through. Empathic people are good listeners and great friends. We all need and appreciate this type of person, for they serve as a kind of "glue" in the team's social structure. Which brings us to . . .

- *Friendship*—Often a child joins a team simply because a friend or friends are on it. No other reason. Likewise, friendships can often be the most influential factor in keeping a child on the team. Many a great athlete has almost quit the sport in which he or she eventually excelled, only to hang in there because of the friendships formed. Numerous are the days where the sheer difficulty or drudgery of practice threatens to bring the athlete down, only to have him or her be picked up by the helpful observations, encouraging words, or even just the mere presence of good friends.

4. Other Talents

Team members may have talents that at first glance have nothing to do with their sport or the team. Special artistic or musical talent might fall into this category. How about a singer for the national anthem? Give me a great writer for any number of team tasks, whether penning inspirational poems or thinking up the lyrics for a rousing cheer. Who better than an artist to take charge of posters and decorations for the big meet? I still have a copy of my 1975 summer swim squad's team logo that went on our banner, T-shirts, awards patches, and so on. It was designed by a fifteen-year-old whose only aquatic skill was a fair breaststroke. I was absolutely floored by his artistic talent when I saw his first rendition. The design featured a smiling, walking star spreading stardust in his wake. Our community and team name was North Star, and the logo was a huge hit, a source of great pride, and a great rallying point for the whole team.

5. Team-Uniting Actions

Oftentimes a team member will advance the cause of his team not because of a quality he possesses, but because of some specific action that he takes that results in positive long-term ramifications for the team. The following is a true story of one such effort. When I was head coach for the New Trier Township High School boys swim team during the early 1980s, there was, among the many truly dedicated athletes on that team, a young man named Jon Nordgren. Jon was one of the best at setting demanding goals for himself and working to exhaustion during the season, all with the objective of achieving big-time drops and swimming his fastest in the key meet or meets at the end of the season. He had a brilliant sophomore season as a JV member, and fully expected to continue that rapid rate of improvement the following winter. Who knows? Maybe he could make the varsity, and just possibly break the magic 50-second mark in his best race, the 100-yard freestyle (his best mark the previous season had been a little over 53 seconds). Jon put even more effort into the sport his junior year, and with barely two weeks to go in the season, he was eagerly anticipating a big payoff to his months of preparation.

It was then that he found out he would be ineligible for the rest of the season due to an insufficient grade point average. Needless to say, Jon was thrown for a loop. His primary focus that winter (swimming and the team) had been taken from him right at the point where all that hard work was going to pay off. Of course the lessons Jon learned from this devastating experience served him well in the future: Studies come first, and one shouldn't ignore that fact in the single-minded pursuit of athletic goals. To his credit, Jon took the news straight up, but he was nonetheless one shattered young man. His teammates rallied around him and assured him they would "win one for Jon," but he still had to face the fact that his season was over. He was neither going to be able to reach his own personal goals or help the team. There would be no closure and no payoff. Or would there?

Jon came up to me a couple of days later and asked for a time trial. This way he could at least find out what he was capable of in his best event, the 100-yard freestyle, while approximating the same conditions he would have encountered had he been able to continue swimming. I was enthusiastic. Frankly, I marveled at his refusal to give up, and thought I saw a way to turn this situation into a positive for the team. We discussed details and agreed to hold the time trial at the end of practice the day before the league championships.

As it worked out, Jon's race would be the first fully tapered performance (the process whereby swimmers reduce their workload, increase their rest, and build their "psyche" toward their final meet) of any of our top-echelon swimmers. My hope was that an exceptional performance by Jon would give confidence to those swimmers uncertain of how their taper would turn out—a sneak preview of things to come for the team. And since taper has such a large mental component, confidence is the key. Have you done the work, and even if you have, will the taper succeed? Just the normal kinds of thoughts swimmers would have around that time of the season. Jon's best time up to that point in the season had been a 52.5 and he was shooting for 50.5. That would be quite a stretch, but if he could pull it off it would put him close to the state-qualifying cut of 49.55, certainly a realistic goal for the following season. But would he be up for this time trial?

The day of Jon's final swim arrived. Our team began a brief practice. I had not seen Jon that day and was a bit worried about how things would turn out. What if he had a mediocre performance? After all, what did he have to swim for? As the team began its final cool down before practice ended I looked around. Still no Jon. We went ahead and began setting up the electronic timing system. Suddenly, the shower door burst open and out strode Jon—minus every hair on his body! (He had "shaved down," a common practice whereby the athlete shaves his/her body hair as a way of reducing drag on the body before the big meet of the season.) All fifty team members went wild, formed a ring around the pool, and began chanting his name. He neither looked right nor left, but merely hopped in, swam a brief warm-up, then jumped up onto the starting blocks. His focus was unwavering as he stared straight ahead, ready for the gun.

The electricity in the air was palpable! We finally got the team calmed down for Jon to hear the commands . . . then the gun went off! Every throat achieved ultra-hoarseness in less than a minute as our squad united in a deafening roar, urging Jon (and the team, for Jon represented all of our highest hopes) onward. What a swim! He was an express train, seeming to gain power and speed as he gobbled up the yards. By the 75-yard mark everyone knew that something momentous was occurring, and that final 25 yards was just a blur of team ecstasy. He hit the wall and turned toward the scoreboard. A split-second hush as everyone craned their necks to see his time . . . 49.49! The place went up for grabs as ecstatic teammates leaped into the water and began pummeling him!

The point had been made: If you had worked hard, your taper would succeed. One week later in the sectionals (the state-qualifying meet), our boys set new team records for both the number of events *and* number of individual swimmers who qualified for the state championships.. Jon's swim was just one event in a long and successful season, but it *surely was a catalyst for our record-breaking team performance.*

Of course, Jon did not score any points in the sectional or state championships, yet it is obvious to me that his performance helped the team score more points than they otherwise would have. In essence, all of the things athletes do and are, as illustrated in our first four categories, have an impact, direct or indirect, on the actual scoring of points. It is, after all, the scoring of points (or runs, touchdowns, goals, etc.) by which team goals are most significantly and easily measured. Simply put, your main team goal is to win and you do that by out- scoring your opponents. Therefore, it's obvious that an athlete who is scoring points is directly helping to achieve his team's key goals.

But what are the factors behind the scenes that helped point-scoring team members score so many points? As a coach you have the opportunity to instill in your athletes the reality that it takes a myriad of talents, skills, and personality types working together to score the greatest number of points. *Give your scorers the credit they are due, but go out of your way to see to it that those less obvious contributions to the team effort are recognized as well.* As a result, your athletes will come to realize that those points up on the board are actually a representation of not only their own efforts, but also those of all of their teammates, coaches, parents, and anyone else that had a positive effect.

"We could not have done as well without you. You could not have done as well without us." That is reality in a true team experience.

Leadership—A Brief Overview

We chose to take on leadership positions by becoming coaches. But do we truly lead? And aren't there many ways to lead, both in substance and in style? In the following section we will delve into this fascinating subject more thoroughly, and it will become rapidly apparent that there is far more to effective leadership than a fiery halftime speech or personally spearheading a charge into enemy lines.

Psychologist Howard Gardner, known for his groundbreaking research on intelligence and leadership, defines a leader as "an individual who significantly affects the thoughts, feelings, and/or behaviors of a significant number of individuals." Those who lead mainly by what they say and how they say it can be termed *direct leaders*. Coaches for the most part are direct leaders. Other examples include heads of state, such as the president and religious leaders such as the pope. People who have mainly influenced others through deed and example, such as cutting edge scientists like Einstein and Newton, are termed *indirect leaders*.

A third category might include those who use a healthy dose of both word and deed to lead. Such examples in the past might include Henry V and Alexander the Great, warrior kings who would fire up their troops with a rousing pre-battle speech, then sally forth at the head of their army. An excellent recent example would be Martin Luther King, one of the leaders and orators of the civil rights movement, who would preach a rousing sermon, then walk at the head of a protest march or lead a sit-in. The great coaches usually exhibit some combination of direct and indirect leadership. Those who are the first to practices and the last to leave, and who are always prepared, *demonstrate* their commitment daily in addition to directly leading.

Leadership—A Combination of Emotional Intelligences

Recent research has confirmed that there are in fact many kinds of intelligence. The common theory used to be that intelligence was measured by SAT scores and IQ tests only. Howard Gardner separates intelligence into seven main categories: (1) spatial capacity (the painter-sculptor Michelangelo, or an architect such as Frank Lloyd Wright), (2) musical (Mozart, Madonna), (3) kinesthetic (displayed in the physical fluidity of dancer Mikhail Baryshnikov or basketball player Michael Jordan), (4) verbal(5) math-logic (these two being the standard academic intelligences), (6) interpersonal skills, and (7) intrapsychic capacity (the ability to be tuned in to one's true feelings).

Gardner freely admits that this number is somewhat arbitrary and that different methods of classification might yield fourteen or even fifty kinds of intelligences, depending on how you break them down. The key point here is that we now recognize there are multiple kinds of intelligences. What is more, the last two types, those Gardner terms personal intelligences, often referred to as people skills, *can be learned and improved upon.* According to Daniel Goleman, author of the groundbreaking book *Emotional Intelligence,* these people skills can be worked on and improved as one gains progressively more understanding of, and control over, one's emotions. This is exciting news for anyone who finds themselves in a leadership position.

One last point before we analyze some principles of leadership: Effective leadership requires both the individual's own leadership capabilities and an understanding of the needs and demands of one's audience. It does no good to develop and use great leadership skills if your cause is not shared or desired by others.

Principles of Leadership

These leadership principles have been gleaned from experts and through experience. They are fairly universal and have stood the test of time.

1. Lead from the front.

Richard Marcinko, in his entertaining book, *Leadership Secrets of the Rogue Warrior,* recounts many amazing experiences leading his troops on forays into the jungles of Vietnam. His role as leader of troops going into battle is perhaps the ultimate example of "leading from the front." Of course, coaching youth basketball teams is not the same as fighting a war. Nevertheless, this principle is universal and applicable for all direct leadership.

You, as the "commander," are asking your fellow coaches and athletes to do some pretty difficult things. If they see you doing the same, either actually or symbolically, your people will more readily perform at a higher level and accomplish more. True, coaches can't do the workouts they ask of their athletes or no coaching would get done, but your athletes will respond to seeing you in the trenches, too, if your work ethic, enthusiasm, and commitment show every day. The message is that you have the same goals and are also working hard to attain them. When you're there everyday before your athletes, when you fashion intelligent lineups and thoughtful workouts, when they see the zeal with which you approach your craft and the importance you ascribe to coaching and to them as individuals, the effect will be as if you're actually doing the workout. Try this sometime: Write the workout on the board and then retreat to your office while your swimmers gamely do their best. They won't, partly because they won't see you and believe *you* are doing *your* best. Nor will they feel you're *with* them, pulling in the same direction together.

Those who "lead from the front" accept responsibility for their own actions and the actions of those they represent. If they are wrong, they admit it. Leaders don't duck, but rather accept responsibility for setbacks, then redouble their efforts toward achieving the goals they and their team have set. "Leadership from the front" also involves vision. This type of leader is forward looking—figuring out the challenges of the future and then creating a plan to meet those new and different challenges.

2. Be aware of your limits.

Don't allow your pride or position to block your awareness of what you know or don't know, or what you can or can't do. In Igor Stravinsky's words, "Awareness of one's ignorance grows exponentially with one's knowledge." Readily admit when you do not have the answer, especially to questions outside your area of expertise, such as what type of injury an athlete might have. Either vow to get the answers or direct your athlete toward a more expert source. In any case, your athletes will respect you more and follow your vision more readily if you're up front about your capabilities and limitations.

3. Demonstrate a willingness to roll up your sleeves. (We're all in this together.)

If you really believe in your cause, you will do whatever it takes to get the job done. If this includes actually doing what the "troops" are doing, then so be it! You are seeing examples of this principle when you see the president of a company stuffing envelopes to help employees meet a mailing deadline, or rolling up his or her sleeves to help out on the assembly line when there is an emergency bottleneck. The message is twofold: First, you're not a prima donna. You may be the person at the top, but that doesn't mean you're above the rest. You recognize that everyone involved has a function, and that just because your position or pay is higher doesn't mean you're superior. As a good leader, you let everyone on the team know they are needed and respected, regardless of rank. Second, you believe in the team's success to a great enough extent that you will do whatever it takes to get the job done. For swim coaches, this may mean getting into the water on a cold day to demonstrate a particular skill. Don't worry about the loss of respect if at times you have to roll up your sleeves. On the contrary, you will gain respect and consequently increase your ability to lead.

4. Treat all with respect.

All humans, whatever age, sex, or race, have value and are to be automatically treated with respect—at least until they show, without a doubt, that they are not to be respected. I cannot overemphasize this point. Assume your athletes are to be respected and your actions will reflect that philosophy. It is amazing what can be accomplished, with willingness and enthusiasm, when those you're leading realize you consider them worthy, valued, and needed. Respect flows both ways, and its presence is an important factor in attaining greater success

5. *Pass around the credit.*

It naturally follows that if you respect your athletes, you want to show that respect by giving credit to anyone deserving it.. We often unintentionally forget to recognize someone's contribution. Make it a priority not only to recognize merit, but also to move mountains to hunt for ways to reward those who don't normally get the credit (e.g., anyone not in your starting lineup). Passing around the credit shows that you truly believe that it takes everyone on the team, each doing his or her best, to achieve your team goals. Your leadership in this regard will help foster this attitude among all your athletes as well.

6. *Treat all equally. (Show no favoritism.)*

Another point that needs to be emphasized—the quickest way to divide and splinter a team is to show favoritism .If you truly value all of your athletes as respected human beings, then you will look for the good points in all of them. This will minimize the tendency to compare and rank them in your mind, which can often result in inadvertent, visible expressions of favoritism. Following the principle of "treating all equally" will also help neutralize the tendency in all of us, for whatever reasons, to be naturally drawn to certain people (and to unintentionally show it). Just remember, to feel that way is one thing, to *show* it is another. Discipline yourself to emphasize the positives in a person, both to the individual and to the group. As a result, you will find that each team member will feel he or she is special to you, and that's the goal here. If your athletes believe you think they are special, they tend not to care *how* special. They do not make comparisons. They don't dwell on rank. There is no negative issue. This principle is fundamental to creating unity within the team.

7. *Lead by action as well as by speech. (Role modeling.)*

The way you act and "are" can be as powerful a statement as what you say. This is true particularly when what you espouse is at odds with your actions. For example, I never want to see my assistant coaches sitting down during practice for any reason. They should be standing up, leaning forward, and moving. I expect them to be physically involved with the practice and the swimmers. Active engagement not only helps the assistants stay more alert and productive, but also sends a message, through their body language, that we're all striving as a group, all working hard toward the common goal. Ask yourself: What is my body saying? Sitting down implies relaxation or laziness. Standing up implies engagement in the workout. Leaning forward signals interest, motivation, and enthusiasm. You would be amazed at the subtle body language signals your athletes sense and interpret as literally as speech.

8. Be athlete oriented.

Remember—you're in it for them, not the other way around. In business parlance, the athlete is your customer, and good leadership always centers on the customer. Get to know your athletes and their goals, so that you can better serve their needs and give them a high-quality experience. In any event, *they are the story—not you.*

▶ Summary Points ▶ ▶ ▶

▶ Teaching young athletes to work together and unite as a team is a challenge coaches face each season. It is also of critical importance to their overall development.

▶ A coach's first step is teaching cooperation among the group members. Step two is to motivate athletes to *want* to strive together as a team and to begin helping each other, which is *teamwork*. *Synergism* is teamwork taken to the *nth* degree, when all involved willingly put all their efforts toward *team* over *individual* success.

▶ *Team building* is the term used to describe a coach's planned actions for building team unity.

▶ Coaches are the team leaders. Their attitude about their athletes and about the importance of team cohesion will therefore set the tone for how united a team becomes. The Foundation Attitudes that form the basis for building team cohesion include: (1) *All athletes have value,* (2) *All are, therefore, important to the team and to you,* and (3) *All deserve respect.*

▶ For older age group athletes, team goal-setting is often the most important team-building and team-uniting activity a coach can initiate. It sets the tone and direction for the group.

▶ Planned activities, such as dinners and fun group outings, are additional ways to bring the group together, no matter what the age, and can often begin before the season commences.

▶ There are many ways athletes contribute value to their teams beyond point-scoring. By showing great effort in practices and in contests and using such positive personal qualities as empathy, enthusiasm, loyalty, and friendship, an athlete can have a tremendously positive effect on overall team success.

4

Competition

The topic of competition in sport is nothing if not controversial. Some claim it builds character and prepares participants for life in contemporary society. Others say competition destroys confidence, creates anxiety, and leads people to value winning over fair play and self-development. These seemingly contradictory viewpoints are both valid, depending on one's history and attitude. However, there is no reason that youngsters can't learn to view competition in a positive light, and as a result grow, learn from, and enjoy most of the competitions they experience. Since we often come across situations in our everyday lives that are competitive in nature, it is critical that youngsters start off right in their outlook toward competition. If coaches make the teaching of a positive competitive attitude a top priority, many long-lasting benefits will accrue.

In this chapter we will examine competition from all sides. How is competition defined? Why is competition so important? How and why is it viewed negatively by some? What are the differences between an adult professional's perspective and that of a child, and what does that tell us about how to approach competition when it comes to coaching young athletes? Finally, the latter portion of this chapter is devoted to defining, understanding, and putting into action a healthy and positive, yet realistic, competitive attitude.

What Is Competition?

The *American Heritage* dictionary defines competition as "a striving or vying with another or others for profit, prize, position, or the necessities of life." Referring specifically to sports, Jay Coakley, author of *Sport in Soci-*

ety(10th Edition (McGraw Hill, 2008), describes competition in sports as "a process through which success is measured by directly comparing the achievements of those who are performing the same physical activity under standardized conditions and rules. [Therefore] competition is a process through which winners and losers are identified based on who does better than whom." We should also recognize that competition exists in other forms as well as between humans. We compete with the elements, animals, time, and quite often ourselves.

A Fact of Life

Competition is a fact of life, a process in which people participate, often willingly, many times throughout their lives. We compete for jobs and blue ribbons; sometimes we race to get the crops in before it storms or sometimes just to be first in line. This fact of life applies to the young as well. Children are constantly testing themselves against others and their surroundings. Can I climb this jungle gym? Who can get to the end of the block first? In many ways, competition serves as a crude but effective way for youngsters to begin sorting out their strengths and weaknesses.

Competition has been ingrained in humans of all ages ever since primitive peoples came on the scene, living among and competing with animals for food and survival. Of course in prehistoric times, competition was essential for survival. Despite our evolution, however, competition remains central to so much of what we do today.

In the United States most sports activities for children are organized as competitions. They run the gamut, from games of baseball to track meets and soccer matches. Most children compete in leagues or other organized groups where results are recorded and standings kept. In schools, students compete for grades and admission into preferred colleges. As adults we must learn to thrive in an economic system where individuals and companies compete with each other to put out the best service or product and are generally rewarded accordingly. Therefore, whether we like it or not, much of our society is structured in competitive terms.

Competition may be pervasive, yet some people are either just not competitive by nature or shy away from such situations for a number of other reasons, such as having had negative childhood experiences, or because of low self-esteem. Even many of those who do embrace competition have mild to severe difficulty in handling it constructively, regardless of outcome. Therefore it's critical for children to develop a healthy understanding and appreciation for the competitive process as early as possible. This is one important way age group coaches can positively influence young lives. After all, everyone has certain strengths and aptitudes which, when tested, will become apparent, so children need to develop the confidence that they will eventually succeed in some arena if they keep trying. Competition is one very important path our young take toward self-discovery and success.

There Is a Process and an Outcome

Referring to our definition, competition involves both a *process* (the contest, the action) and an *outcome* (the result). I believe that the heart and soul of competition exists in the process, where the fun, excitement, and (viewing it from a coaching or parenting perspective) main potential for growth lie. Unfortunately, in American society we too often focus primarily on the outcome. For example, the first words out of a parent's mouth when his or her child comes home from an athletic contest often are— "Did you win today?"

During a contest, athletes do not know the outcome and are exerting themselves to the utmost, making their best attempt to positively affect the end result. That *doing* is where the joy resides. It is also where young athletes learn to accept challenges and try their best while building confidence. Competition also leads to self-discovery—finding out what strengths and aptitudes one possesses. But all these positives can be compromised when a coach makes too big a deal over the "W" or "L". Therefore, when developing a Healthy Competitive Attitude (detailed later in this chapter), the first step for all coaches should be to emphasize the competing to the best of one's abilities and how fun and rewarding that is, and not to unduly hype the result.

Why Do Some See Competition as a Negative?

The *act* of competing is neither good nor bad. It just *is*. Why, then, do some view competition so negatively? As previously noted, a large share of the blame must go to the many parents and coaches who view winning as the only worthwhile result. Their disproportionate focus on the importance of the outcome places excessive negative pressure on young athletes, who in turn conclude that competition is fraught with too much downside and is just no fun. Another significant negative factor often occurs when coaches and competitors display that "win at all costs" attitude. It often materializes as yelling at athletes, taunting opponents, breaking rules, and other inappropriate behaviors. For many, this excessive exposure to unhealthy competitive attitudes and experiences at a young age forever casts an indelible cloud over competing.

The fact is, how we view competition will determine whether there'll be a positive, neutral, or negative spin placed on any contended event. If children learn that it's always "us against them" and that they have to win or feel like a loser, then they will most likely develop a rather grim view of all competition—that it's a "war" with a huge downside, and that one must win or else retire from the field of combat in shame. No wonder many of our young feel so much stress! However, if a coach's message to the athletes is that contests are an exciting opportunity to test oneself, that the other person or team is an opponent and not "the enemy," and that the emphasis is on improvement over result, then that coach will be inculcating and reinforcing a healthy, positive competitive attitude in his or her athletes, both toward their sport and toward anything else life can throw at them. Moreover, the focus on process frees athletes psychologically to learn and grow from each competitive experience, which is what all coaches want from their athletes. When reviewing their performance after each race, I ask athletes what they did especially well as well as what they learned. If the athlete only cares about the result, their caring, and therefore insight into *how* they performed, technically, strategically, and otherwise, will be reduced, and an opportunity to learn and grow will be limited or not occur at all.

Competition is pervasive in our society and often becomes more central to our quality of life the older we get (college entrance, jobs, wages). We have a golden opportunity with our very young to school them in a constructive, positive, yet realistic view of competition and help them handle victory, defeat, success, and disappointment.

Winning and Losing: The Difference in Emphasis Between the Young Amateur and the Adult Professional

One reason many youth coaches excessively emphasize outcome may be due to ignorance of the huge difference between pro sports (what we read about and follow so much as a society) and youth sports. As a result, they have too often used the professional sports philosophy—that winning is the only thing that matters—as a model for guiding children. Nothing could be less appropriate.

Vince Lombardi, former coach of the perennial pro football champions, the Green Bay Packers, once declared, "Winning isn't everything, it's the only thing." I presume he was talking about paid athletes and the necessity for single-minded devotion to what really is the only goal in professional sports—winning. Considered in the context of a paid adult doing a job, this is a reasonable statement. After all, in the business world, it is either produce or find another line of work. However, professional athletes are better prepared to deal with the premium placed on winning. They have chosen that particular sport above all other possible vocations as their life's work. Since they are adults with years of experience in that field, they should possess enough physical and mental maturity to handle the often constant criticism and the ups and downs of their sport. Moreover, pro athletes are expected to work hard at practice and produce at games because they are getting paid to do so. Yet, as previously noted, there is a world of difference between age group athletes and adults when it comes to ability and experience, self-esteem and levels of awareness, and goals and aspirations. The child athlete is still developing—physically, mentally, emotionally, and socially. He or she is still discovering strengths and weaknesses, likes and dislikes. His or her sense of self is evolving, and the athlete is emotionally far more tender than an adult professional. For these reasons alone the young should be coached to improve and not merely to win, meaning age group coaches must work hard to balance properly the emphasis between process and outcome.

Children have a different perspective than adults when it comes to what's important in competitions. The younger the child, the greater are those differences. For instance, while adults focus more on the bottom line, children in primary school concern themselves with participation and having fun. Many years ago I ran across a study done with seven- and eight-year-olds that concluded over 90 percent would prefer to play on a losing team rather than ride the bench on a winning team! Further, 95 percent of those surveyed *would rather have fun than worry about winning*! My own observations since then only bear this out. True, younger children do care about the outcome, but not nearly to the same extent as teenagers, and nowhere near the all-or-nothing ethos inherent in professional sports.

Without question, youth sports is a very different animal than pro sports, and, therefore, should be coached accordingly. Emphasis should be placed on the development of the child, and not solely on seeing who can achieve the best won/lost record.

The Striving to Win Still Has Its Place

One might infer from the previous section that I think winning should not be a priority in youth sports. This is not the case. What *is* critical when coaching age group sports is to keep winning in perspective. While the goal of winning is and should be a priority (the amount of emphasis depending on the age of the athletes),the actual striving toward, and handling of, winning and losing is of even greater importance. Assuming the athlete has that perspective, the concentration of mind and body toward winning is positive in many ways.

Why should coaches place importance on the goal of winning? First, winning is an obvious and notable objective for athletes in individually-oriented sports such as wrestling and track, where numerous individual matches and races add up to team results. Second, and more significantly, the *striving* to outpoint the other team (in a dual meet, match, or game) or to place as high as possible (in tournaments involving many teams) is the most clear-cut and meaningful goal for the team. Why? Because team score is *the embodiment of the group's united efforts.* Additionally, the value of winning as a goal for age group athletes is that it teaches them to focus their mental and physical powers on attaining an important objective. They are learning how to succeed by whatever measure.

Many have heard the phrase "success is a journey." Put another way, success is a whole series of efforts toward betterment, with some victories and defeats along the way, always aimed at a higher level of prowess and achievement. That constant striving for excellence is "the big picture," for what ultimately matters is the kind of person the child turns out to be.

An eight-year-old boy starting his first year in soccer discovers that he loves the sport. He begins a "journey" toward a level of excellence that may eventually reach a high school, college, or (in rare cases) professional career many years later. It will take him through literally thousands of practice sessions and hundreds of matches. *How he takes that journey, whether he learns to—*

- *play by the rules,*
- *respect his teammates, the opposition, and officials,*
- *sacrifice for the team,*
- *constantly strive to improve, and*
- *give everything he has toward the accomplishment of his and his team's objectives*

is of far greater import than the results of any single contest.

William Warren, author of the book *Coaching and Motivation* (Reedswain Publishing, 2002), upon coming to the realization that his 14–9 basketball team was far more enjoyable to coach than the previous year's 25–2 squad, observed that "I'd rather lose . . . with players who are willing to run into walls for the team, than to win every day with more talented youngsters who don't care about each other . . . victory isn't what shows up on the scoreboard . . . it's what shows up in a youngster's heart, as evidenced by the manner in which he/she plays the game."

The acquisition of these success habits and lessons by the young athlete will occur, slowly but surely, over the course of countless practices, contests, even seasons. *But these habits will take hold*, and will stay with them forever, if you, the coach, keep winning and losing in perspective and coach the athletes accordingly.

The Value of Losing

Inevitably, portions of any path to excellence will include frustrations, setbacks, and losses, both personal and team-based. However, a loss will motivate determined athletes by stiffening their resolve to apply themselves even more vigorously toward the goal not yet reached. Secondly, a loss can serve as effectively as a win when monitoring progress ("We gave our favored opponent all they could handle. I and my teammates worked together more cohesively than we thought we could, and it shows me that we are ahead of schedule.").

Perhaps the most valuable function of losing is in giving the young athlete the opportunity to experience—and learn how to handle—the downs as well as the ups in any situation. Recognizing and coming to terms with the reality that athletes don't always win will actually *aid* their ability to compete at a consistently higher level. They will not be hamstrung, for example, by the fear of losing, causing an apprehension that can tighten muscles and force thoughts toward the negative. Phil Jackson, coach of numerous National Basketball Association (NBA) champion teams, observes in his book *Sacred Hoops* that, "As strange as it may seem, being able to accept change or defeat with equanimity gives you the freedom to… give the game your all."

Ultimately, young athletes need to be reminded that losing does not mean that you are a loser, just as winning does not necessarily make you a winner. Yes, winning is an admirable goal, and to win is surely satisfying and a lot of fun. However, the *commitment to*, and the *effort applied toward* winning or any other goal is what truly makes us successful and is an important concept for young athletes to learn.

A Healthy Competitive Attitude

Approached in the right way, any type of competition can be motivational, tremendously productive, and exhilarating. Since competition is so common in our society, it is critical that we get young people on the right track from the start in their attitudes toward it. The key to maximizing the positive benefits of competition while minimizing the negative is the development of a healthy competitive attitude. Preschool and elementary school teachers and age group coaches are usually the first adult influences, other than parents, to spend meaningful amounts of time with our youth. Of these, coaches have perhaps the purest vehicle—a competitive sports team—with which to expose young athletes to these values.

There are several important principles, detailed below, that form a healthy competitive attitude. They need to be taught, modeled, and constantly reinforced before a coach can expect such values to be consistently demonstrated by his or her athletes while competing.

The following principles outline a view of competition that is positive yet realistic. Young athletes who embrace this view will get so much more out of their age group sports experience, both immediately and in the long term. In the following five sections each principle is defined and its long-term benefits described. Teach this philosophy to your athletes, and then reinforce it through your words and actions every chance you get.

1. Competition Is a Process and an Outcome: Embrace the Process!

The process is the game itself (the action, the effort), which inevitably leads to a result (a win or loss). The outcome helps give a contest framework and meaning, but its importance is relative and must be determined by the athletes themselves. Emphasize to young athletes the contest over the outcome. Help develop in them a love and desire for the act of competing. Teach them to embrace the process by always giving it their best shot while at the same time enjoying the game.

As for results, recognize their importance but put them in perspective. Explain exactly why the outcome *is* of great importance, but that there will be days when they win, and days they won't. In any event an age group athlete's ultimate, overriding, long-term focus is on improving in all ways, and these contests are periodic, fun tests of how they are progressing.

An integral part of "the process" is the frequent practice sessions performed in preparation for competition. When we talk of contests and competitions, we are usually referring to the official game, meet, or match. Yet an athlete competes in practice all the time, both with teammates and within himself or herself. The stakes aren't quite as high, but it's happening there on a constant basis, and of course the principles that delineate a healthy competitive attitude apply in the practice arena as well.

Incidentally, balancing practice sessions within the competition schedule is another way for you to help create success. In practice, athletes prepare for a contest. During practice they make adjustments to continue improving themselves between competitions. When possible, I like to space out our swim meets for precisely that reason. I want our athletes to have sufficient practice time between meets to give them the best chance possible to show visible and/or measurable improvement in as many contests as possible. The amount of time needed will differ among the various sports and age groups, and even from athlete to athlete within the same age group. However, if you have some control over your schedule and can intelligently space your competitions, your athletes will feel successful more often; not because they won or not, but because they worked hard, improved, and then demonstrated their improvement to parents, teammates, coaches, and, most important, to themselves.

Long-term benefits: Placing the importance of the outcome in proper perspective reduces the fear of failure so many young athletes experience. When they begin to comprehend the notion that we can all be winners in the broader sense, they get a powerful boost to their confidence and self-esteem.

From the standpoint of effort, putting a premium on the contest as opposed to the outcome also teaches a child to do his or her best under *all* circumstances. That is an important message longer term because life is not so cut and dried. What dominates is the daily struggle. The person who applies himself or herself consistently will inevitably succeed more often and reach his or her goals.

Practice is where young athletes develop the habits of success that will enable them to put their best foot forward. Habits such as punctuality, regular attendance, and persistent effort despite fatigue or other setbacks, as well as qualities such as accepting responsibility and sacrificing self-interest for the greater good (team, family, company) are learned and developed during practice sessions.

It's possible that the greatest benefits to experiencing the competitive process are psychological. When practice and hard work lead to achievement, children come to *really believe* that hard work leads to positive results, and that they have the power to effect that change themselves. The process, which involves many small, measured steps, builds in the child the sense that "if I stick with something, I can do it!" Many times parents have related to me how their sons or daughters were transformed from strugglers into superior students when they started applying themselves in school as a direct result of experiencing success through hard work in a sport. When they learn to believe in their own power to affect change, their confidence shoots skyward, and performance in any endeavor is enhanced.

All the preceding benefits directly contribute to heightened self-esteem. Nothing is more important to the growth of an individual than the early development of a healthy, positive sense of oneself.

2. There Is a Winner and a Loser in Virtually All Competitions

Included in the rules of any competition are the ones that decree who wins (the fastest, the most points, etc.) and who doesn't. Have your athletes realize that in that specific sense they will be one or the other on any given day and accept whatever the outcome with good grace. However, make them aware that in a broader sense we are all winners if we give our best effort, both mentally and physically, honor the opposition, compete fairly, accentuate the positive, and handle the outcome with grace and dignity.

Long-term benefits: By placing winning and losing in the proper context, by constantly encouraging athletes to participate for all the positive reasons, and by positively reinforcing them for doing so, you will be creating the type of environment in which children will want to take part. They will develop an increased appreciation and enjoyment for competition that will last their entire lives.

3. Improvement Is the Overriding, Long-Term Focus

Improvement is the number one priority for an age group coach—improvement of each athlete, as well as that of the team as a unit. Great records and trophies are merely by-products of improvement. Young athletes should be acknowledged when they make headway. They should be taught that all competitions are opportunities for them to show their progress, and that the process of improving never ends. There is always something to work on!

Long-term benefits: Focusing on improvement, which generally occurs incrementally (see "Goal Setting" in Chapter Two), helps children develop productive practice habits and reinforces in them the concepts of discipline and perseverance. We should inculcate in our charges that a disciplined, consistent practice approach is required to fuel the steady engine of progress, and that greater success will come to those who stay the course. To aid in this learning process, a coach should make it a priority to help athletes identify and appreciate their most incremental of improvements, thereby reinforcing what a disciplined approach accomplishes. By pointing out when an athlete improves (and it will happen quite often and sometimes dramatically with a youth new to the sport), a coach can give frequent, positive feedback, thereby motivating the child to strive for improvement and continue to want to persevere.

4. There Are Many Ways to Measure Success

While the final score is a very important measure of success, there are other measures that are vitally important to attaining accomplishment—time drops, points scored, and advances in technique offer a few of the valuable measuring sticks at hand. When athletes realize these measures help paint a picture of improvement and success, they often feel relieved of the pressure of always having to win. When the coach realizes there are countless ways to assess progress, innumerable motivational doors open up. Fortunately, all sports have their own unique aspects that can be measured either by time, by tape measure, or just by the naked eye. Some of the methods I have found useful in swimming include the following:

> *Times:* Even if Sue comes in 12th out of 12, did she improve on her previous best time? If she competed in a longer race where strategy dictates going faster at certain points in the race, did she improve her times during those key portions of the race)? After having made some mistakes during a race earlier in the meet, did she swim the same race faster or freer of mistakes the second time? After having swum five races, run to the pharmacy two miles away and back to grab medicine for an asthmatic teammate, and lifted the front end of a car to save her grandmother trapped underneath, did she still do a respectable time on the last relay?
>
> Best times often occur sporadically. When there is nothing, time-wise, that you can comment on favorably, you can always measure success and improvement in other ways.

Technique: Did John execute his backstroke start correctly? Effectively? Was his form correct when using the new breaststroke technique he had been working on all week? Chances are that initially John may have gone slower with this new technique. Even though his form may have been right on, it sometimes takes a while for a swimmer's feel, that grip on the water, to come back. In this case measuring John's progress either by his placement in the event or by time would have completely missed the success he experienced.

Effort: How about Dana's gutsy finish as she came from way behind in the last two lengths to nip her rival and get the key third place point the team needed? It was neither first place nor her best time, but best times don't occur every day, and with a true team effort the third places are sometimes as important as the firsts. Or what about young Tom, who swam his first butterfly race after having just learned the stroke a few days before? He barely finished, and had to be helped from the pool, but he did it. And then there is Sonia, who is not even close to being the most talented member of the team, but who sprints most of the workout almost every day. Her teammates are challenged and motivated by her example to pick up the pace, which makes them practice faster, which results in faster times and higher placements at meets for the entire team.

Teamwork and sacrifice: Leading organized cheers at meets, making motivational posters for teammates, handling with equanimity being replaced in the lineup at the last minute—all successes in my book. How about Graham, who has to swim his two poorest events because the team needs him there? Though he knows he won't show as well as he usually does, and is totally unprepared because his coach never has him practice those events, he still gives his best with a smile and zero complaints. A huge success.

Long-term benefits: Accepting the concept that there are many ways of measuring success allows one to be more realistic and honest in evaluating any endeavor. Here is an example from the business world: Doreen is newly hired at the local brokerage. Her boss gives her a list of potential customers she must cold-call. She makes ninety calls that day, a Friday. Fifty do not answer, thirty hang up on her, and of the remaining ten, only two agree to a personal visit. Is Doreen a success? Two out of ninety? And no actual sales? Sounds like almost total failure. But Doreen re-evaluates her performance and discovers that she only made sixty calls the previous day, so her effort is up, and whereas all but one hung up on Thursday, she got ten to actually have a conversation with her on Friday, which could mean her message is becoming more polished. Compared with her previous day's performance, Doreen judges her day a success.

5. Your Opponent Is Not "the Enemy"!

Quite the opposite is true. An opponent invariably helps improve one's own performance. Therefore, *welcome* any competition for the motivating force it is. For example, our summer swim team had time trials (timed races between team members at a practice or other non-meet session) about one week before its first meet each summer. One summer, out of curiosity, I did a test of 13 seven- and eight year-old girls (our "Eight and Under" group). They had practiced for three weeks before the timing period. Each of them was timed in a 25-yard freestyle:

- in a solo trial, that is, no one raced them;

- at the team time trials, where there were usually five teammates racing at a time;

- at their first dual meet (a "dual" between two teams), held a few days after the team time trials.

- All three sets of times occurred less than a week apart, so potential improvement from practicing was minimal at best. Here were the results:

	Solo Trial	Team Trial	Dual Meet
Average Time	26.0	22.2	20.6

Since that test I have watched scores of youngsters go through the same series of tests and found that in virtually all cases the same general result occurs. Without question, having an opponent to race with aids performance greatly (in addition, the more importance placed on the opponent, the better the performances; hence, the faster swims versus other teams instead of versus their own teammates). Moreover, the closer in ability that opponent is, the better the performance will tend to be. The same increase in effort and overall performance will be true in any sport, whether it manifests itself in catching tougher passes (football), executing difficult dives more flawlessly (diving), or reeling off faster splits (marathon running).

A Healthy Competitive Attitude in Action

As your athletes acquire a solid understanding of what a healthy competitive attitude is, their actions will start to reflect that philosophy. Help them by explaining and reinforcing how they should comport themselves while in action.

1. Give It Your Best Effort

"Honor thy competition and thyself" by striving to do your very best always, both mentally and physically. Also recognize that certain competitions can be daunting; at times it takes real courage just to take on that challenge. Be strong, follow through, and give yourself credit for having done so.

Part of honoring the competition is in knowing when your opponent has been defeated and showing restraint at that time. I don't mean a team should lie down. Through lineup changes, play calling, and other methods, the coach can change the team's strategy from *focus-on-victory* to *focus-on-improvement* (the victory goal having been assured). It serves no good purpose to rub the loser's nose in it, such as when one team piles on the score in a game long since decided.

By the way, it's interesting to note that younger children, when left to their own devices, tend to seek out close competition. Growing up and playing sandlot baseball and football, I can remember countless times when the sides were unfair and we would stop everything and simply revamp the teams precisely to create a more competitive situation. Giving both teams an equal chance made the game more fun.

2. Treat Your Opponents with Respect

Be courteous and honorable. Neither negative actions, such as cheap shots, nor negative words, such as putdowns or slurs, have any place on the field of competition ("trash talking" in young people is a reflection of poor character and stems from a lack of respect). Be true to the essence of sportsmanship by demonstrating a commitment to the rules, and respect and a lack of animosity toward opponents.

3. Compete Within the Rules

Rules provide the framework within which we compete. Without rules the game would be utter chaos—no rhyme or reason, and no fun. After all, the fun is in contesting the opposite side within guidelines both sides understand and agree to.

The officials in any contest are the upholders of the rules, sometimes a thankless task. Frequently, we target officials with negative attention, such as when there's a dispute, or possibly a missed call. But, as coaches, we must teach our athletes that the officials are to be treated with the utmost respect and that their final word on any issue is just that, *final*. Of course, there will be times when you owe it to your team to point out an apparent injustice or seek clarification on a certain ruling. By handling those situations in a respectful, diplomatic fashion, you will be modeling the very type of attitude and behavior toward officials that you want your athletes to emulate.

4. Accentuate the Positive

Show genuine appreciation toward your teammates, not only for outstanding performances, but for their general efforts as well. Be upbeat. Enjoy the fresh air, the audience excitement, and the intensity of the game. Take it all in and revel in it! Putdowns, criticisms, berating of umpires and of the opposition, and other negative actions will tend to detract from your performance, bring down your teammates, and negatively affect the quality of your experience.

5. Accept the Result Gracefully

Young athletes often have a difficult time experiencing loss. After all, it's easy to acknowledge victory, but do not forget to be gracious. It's tougher to handle losing with dignity. You might feel like lashing out, throwing things, or blaming yourself (or others), yet those actions do nothing but dishonor you and your opposition. Instead:

- Accept the loss for what it is—disappointing. You gave it your best shot and came up a bit short.

- Don't make excuses. If the communication can be given and received in a genuine fashion, congratulate your opponent. In any event, they were the better team that day.

- Learn whatever you can from the defeat and vow to work on those areas you identify as being in need of improvement.

- Then… get to work! Use the losses, as well as the wins, as yardsticks of progress and as motivation to do better, not as roadblocks or excuses to quit. Identify major areas in need of strengthening, set goals designed to guide that improvement, and get to it!

An underlying feeling of satisfaction occurs after any competition when real progress occurs after such steps are taken. In any event, the long-term focus remains on improvement.

The Fruits of Embracing a Healthy Competitive Attitude

Will athletes who develop a healthy competitive attitude be more successful as measured by traditional means? Absolutely. They have learned valuable lessons about dealing with people and have developed qualities such as discipline and perseverance. They will most definitely be more positive, understanding, and forgiving during competitions than those who don't embrace such an attitude. Ultimately, the athlete will be more open to all the good things a competitive experience has to offer.

Many of our team parents have told me that, for their child, the benefits of swimming extend well beyond the pool. Along with increased physical fitness and success in the pool, their children developed discipline, an improved ability to organize, learned how to set realistic yet challenging goals and then follow through with the appropriate effort, and developed an increased self-confidence and courage in risk-taking. Equally important, children experienced the social aspects of leadership, teamwork, support of friends, and sacrificing for others. Sports can be such an amazing vehicle for overall growth. A youngster's development of a healthy competitive attitude is one big step in his or her evolution that coaches can be of assistance with.

A Case Study: The Greatest Race

Mighty Mill Valley versus South Bay. Mill Valley, last year's champions and odds-on favorite to repeat, was facing the rapidly improving South Bay upstarts in the last dual meet of another intense summer swim season. Both clubs had arrived undefeated for the season at the scene of the contest, the South Bay pool. South Bay knew it would take a perfect meet to overcome Mill Valley, and the meet so far had lived up to all the anticipation—fiercely contested races, and upsets and surprises on both sides. The crowd roared at every race, and the atmosphere was electric along both sidelines as two sky-high teams duked it out that sunny Saturday morning. Yet despite South

Bay's finest efforts, Mill Valley's superiority was beginning to assert itself. Whereas lead changes were numerous during the first twenty events (of 72), by event No. 45 the Valley had assumed a slight but consistent 15- to 20-point edge (over 500 points are typically scored in such a dual meet). By event No. 62 the advantage was 28 points, and a subtle but unmistakable air of inevitability had descended over the proceedings.

This was the setting as event No. 62 was called to the blocks—the 18-and-Under Boys 100-Yard Breaststroke, the last event before the freestyle relays wrapped up the meet. Swimming for Mill Valley in lane three was huge Tom "Terminator" O'Connell, last year's runner up in this event at the league championships. To his right, in lane four, speedy Eddie Morgan, the previous season's 14-and-under champion, now a full six inches taller. Facing these two behemoths in lane two was South Bay's lone representative, a slight 15-year-old named Pete Sanderson, who had never made it to the championships in any event in his entire swimming career. This Sanderson was definitely not a star, and had every right to be petrified.

Like many older swimmers in the league, Pete knew his competition. In this case he knew both Terrible Tom and Fast Eddie had 5 inches, 40 pounds, and 6 seconds on him. He also knew his event was one of the few weak links in an otherwise consistently strong South Bay lineup. With his team already down by 28, things did not look promising for South Bay!

But, for some reason, Pete wasn't crumbling under the pressure. Yes, he was aware that his chances were slim. He was nervous, no question. Yet, for the first time in his life, he wasn't obsessing about the opposition. Instead, Pete was focused on how he was going to swim his own race, and he was psyched. He had been working for two weeks on the correct timing of his stroke. Before, when he swam this race, he had looked as if he were furiously stirring a cauldron of soup (and consequently wearing down by the final lap). Pete's new coach, Jumbo Jefferson, had worked tirelessly with Pete on maintaining the correct timing of his arms and legs. The key to Pete's race, Coach Jefferson felt, was not only establishing the correct stroke rhythm, but also in maintaining that rhythm throughout the entire 100 yards. Coach Jefferson would say, "Rhythm is everything in breaststroke," and "When you tire, your timing will tend to break down, causing you to look like a frantic water spider, all constant motion and going nowhere fast."

This rhythm stuff was all new to Pete, and he was eager to try it out in a major competition. As he stepped up to the blocks his dominant thoughts were of race strategy, stroke efficiency, and excitement, not of getting blown away. And though to the audience this seemed a mismatch, Pete felt unusually confident.

The swimmers took the blocks, the gun went off, and immediately the Mill Valley boys asserted themselves. But Pete slipped into and maintained his new super-efficient stroke, and as he neared the first turn he noted through his peripheral vision that—hold the phones!—he was in the thick of it! What's more, his stroke felt unbelievable! He was in a zone he had never experienced before. At the 50-yard mark he and Tom were matching stroke for stroke, with Fast Eddie having fallen slightly off the pace. The crowd's cheers spurred them on as the intrepid aquanauts headed for the third turn...and the cheers turned into a deafening roar as suddenly Superfast Eddie came out of nowhere and all three hit the 75-yard mark simultaneously! It was bedlam as they headed for home. Pete was tiring, but he disciplined his body to maintain that all-important stroke timing as they all strained through the last length, neck and neck. He gamely hung on, but the more powerful Mill Valley duo began inexorably inching ahead. The crowd screaming as they neared the finish . . . then, the final three strokes!

The Mill Valley boys had edged a half-body length ahead with eight yards to go, but they were running out of gas, and fast. The pace had taken them by surprise, and their strokes began to disintegrate as their weary arms seized up. In those final three strokes Pete closed in....pulled closer still... then gave a final powerful kick as he timed the last forward thrust of his arms to reach the wall at full extension even as his rivals, whose bodies were still inches ahead, were forced to do a short extra pull. All three hit the wall in a cloud of spray. Too close to call! A hush, then an incredible roar erupted as the finish judge unhesitatingly stabbed his finger at Pete. "First place!" he bellowed. "This one's first!" The South Bay fans went wild as his teammates mobbed Pete "the Ecstatic." The young upstart had just dropped four full seconds and, unbelievably, had kept South Bay in the meet.

All the preceding events actually did occur. For you strategy buffs, South Bay was down only 27 points after the race. The remaining events were relays and all scored 7–0. So instead of having to win nine of the remaining ten events to win the meet had he finished second or third, Pete's stunning upset put his team in a position to need just seven victorious relays to achieve a win. Still quite a challenge, but definitely possible. Anything could happen!

If young Pete had not had a healthy competitive attitude, he most likely would have never really tried to win; he would have given up instead. According to conventional wisdom, there was no way he had a chance. How many times have we all faced such insurmountable odds, been psychologically beaten down, and not been able to do our best? If we were honest with ourselves we would admit that we more or less gave up. We went through the motions, behavior which is certainly more the norm than the exception. But Pete focused only on the positive, on his race, and he gave it everything he had. He had learned to love competition because he had learned to embrace all the positives, minimize the negative elements, and accept the result, whatever it might have been. Consequently, Pete was able to free up all his capabilities and turn them loose in action. He could truly do his absolute best.

This narrative is just one, albeit fairly dramatic, example of the kind of fun competition can be. Competition is not only about the winning, but about the excitement and the possibilities inherent in challenges as well. Every contest is an opportunity—to test oneself, to improve, to shine. The possibility of doing something wonderful, something you have never done, is a spur that motivates us to try, then try harder.

The young man we know here as Pete actually had a long and varied athletic career, spanning two decades. Amazingly, of the hundreds of competitions in which he was involved, from Little League baseball to college wrestling, this seemingly insignificant summer swim race was quite possibly his most memorable, which points to a critical aspect we coaches should never underestimate or forget. No matter at what level an athlete participates, *what he or she is doing at that time is more important to that athlete than anything else*. Though the league meet that summer was about as far from the Olympics as you can get, Pete was surely as proud of his achievement as any Olympic athlete would be of their gold medals.

Success is relative; improvement as well. Both must be measured within the framework of an athlete's skill and experience level because at that time, and at that level, what the athlete is trying to accomplish is the most important thing in his or her life. For instance, we may at times pay a little less attention to junior varsity athletes and their performances than the varsity's, or we may gloss over exhibition performances to focus on the upcoming "official" event. Yet second string and novice athletes deserve just as much attention from coaches as their more accomplished teammates.

This dictum is especially meaningful when talking about improvement. Progress is relative to the athlete's previous level of performance, not to a teammates' level. Put another way, just as much praise and attention should be lavished on the novice swimmer who goes from a 45.6 to a 43.5 in the 50-yard freestyle as on an Olympic sprinter dropping to a 19.0 from a 19.2 in the same event. Coaches who embrace this reality will find they get much more out of their struggling athletes, and will be able to understand, motivate, and appreciate all their athletes to a far greater extent.

▸ **Summary Points** ▸ ▸ ▸

▸ Coaches have a wonderful opportunity to help show and define for young athletes a view of competition that is fun, positive, and educational.

▸ In a civilized society, youngsters should learn to view competition as a striving *with*, rather than *against*.

▸ Competition is a fact of life, therefore developing a positive competitive attitude while learning how to enjoy and gain from competition should be paramount in a child's education.

▸ Competition involves both a *process* (the contest) and an *outcome* (the result). Focusing more on the process is central to building a positive competitive attitude.

▸ Winning and losing should be secondary objectives for the very young athlete. It is the doing that is most important. This equation gradually shifts as children move into middle, then high school.

▸ Winning, and the striving toward it, is important! The goal of winning is the single most important and uniting goal a team has. It sums up what all the group's united efforts are about, and through that striving, individuals and the team learn success habits that will stay with them throughout their life, however . . .

▸ Learning how to handle defeat (with grace, dignity, and respect for teammates and opponents) as well as learning what losing teaches the athlete (about weaknesses and strengths, about character, etc.) show why coming up short in a contest can often be as positive *developmentally* as winning!

▶ A Healthy Competitive Attitude should include:

Embracing the process over the outcome.

Recognizing that there is a winner and loser, but never stop trying!

Focusing on improvement as a constant and long-term strategy.

▶ A Healthy Competitive Attitude in Action involves:

a. Giving it one's all, always.

b. Treating one's opponents and the referees with respect.

c. Competing within the rules.

d. Accentuating the positive, within oneself and toward one's teammates, in all one does during competition.

e. Accepting the result in a dignified, respectful manner.

▶ The "Law of Relativity" means that, relatively speaking, an athlete's first soccer goal ever is as important to her at that instant in her life as an Olympian's achieving her first gold medal is to her.

Coaching Techniques

• •

What kinds of words, actions, and methods are most effective when coaching your athletes? What are great ways to command attention, to get across information clearly yet quickly, to inspire, to nurture, to discipline? We have already covered many aspects of coaching, and peppered throughout are practical "how to's." Here we will more comprehensively examine the planning of practices and contests that have the best chance for success, as well as words, actions, non-actions, and other methods that help a coach operate most effectively. But first let's remind ourselves of what the goal of all our efforts is.

The Goal

Being the best we can be as coaches involves attention to the key aspects of coaching—helping athletes improve in their chosen sport and evolve as individuals while having as high quality an experience as possible. When setting performance objectives for themselves, coaches should look past the results their teams achieve and ask themselves, How effectively do I teach and motivate?

1. **Quality of Teaching and Motivating Objective:** The more knowledgeable a coach is, the more knowledge he or she potentially can impart to the athlete. However, there is no guarantee that knowledge will be conveyed well. Top-level coaching involves the transmission of that knowledge effectively, so that it is both *received* and *retained*. Moreover, the best coaches are able to inspire their athletes to want to learn more and be more successful. Many of the

techniques found in this chapter will aid any coach in becoming better teachers, organizers, and motivators, resulting in their athletes improving more quickly.

Setting and achieving performance goals is central to a coach's improving his or her skills as a coach. But guiding their actions is their big-picture philosophy about their role vis-à-vis the athletes. Coaches need to ask themselves: how do you view your job? Or more specifically, how much effort do you put into helping your athletes evolve as individuals and how much attention do you spend toward making the overall experience as high-quality as possible?

2. **High Quality of Life Objective:** Coaches fall into three main camps with respect to how they view their vocations:

   - Economic Objective *(It's a Job)*. Coaches who view their position this way are in it more for the economic benefits than anything else. They are mainly punching a clock. Not a lot of passion, few goals. It's just a job.

   - Conventional Objective *(the Results Coach)*. This is the way, I believe, that most people view coaching. Coaches who fit into this category look on their job, in the main, as improving their athletes vis-à-vis their sport. That is, goals are usually set and passion is often exhibited, but the focus of these coaches is relatively narrow. Results such as wins, points, and placement are their overriding measurements of success. *How* results are achieved is secondary to the fact that they are achieved. This doesn't mean that Results Coaches aren't sensitive to how sports benefit the child in other ways, or that they aren't often the greatest of people (which so many are). Merely that Results Coaches don't measure the success of their program in broader, life experience kinds of ways. This Conventional Objective has been the most widely accepted "mission statement" of our vocation, but, in my opinion, is far too narrow. We are supposed to make Johnny a better soccer player, Mary a finer gymnast. But does Mary love practices, her teammates, the process? Does Johnny learn about teamwork, sacrifice, and commitment, and how those attributes can positively affect other areas of his life? The Conventional View recognizes that those benefits may occur, but results (improved skills, more wins) are the only real measuring stick of that program's or that child's success. Since helping the person (child, adolescent, teenager) evolve is at least as important as, and inextricably intertwined with, improving the athlete's skills and performance, it is my hope that more and more coaches will embrace the more holistic view of their job, that is, the High Quality of Life Objective.

- High Quality of Life Objective. The focus in this instance is a dual one—helping athletes grow as people while helping them improve in their sport. The coaching of a sport is a vehicle for teaching life-lessons. What's more, practices are conducted in ways that provide numerous opportunities for athletes to be successful, and in ways that are exciting and fun. The athlete develops a powerful *want*—to be at practices and games, and to improve. Great results are the *outcome* of a culture of hard work, high expectations, and a united commitment to excellence. Moreover, the learning of *how* to succeed (and fail, for that matter) is as important as the succeeding. The creation of strong, positive coach athlete connections is at the heart of such a program since such a relationship reflects the coach's deep commitment to the athlete and because such a positive connection will only aid in achieving a high-quality experience for both coach and athlete. When a coach operates such a program, not only are all accomplishing a lot, but also coaches and athletes love what they do, love the process, and love coming to practice. Inevitably, many, if not most, athletes in such a program become self-motivated, which is what we all want our athletes to achieve.

I believe coaches should be able to effectively teach and motivate, resulting in tremendous improvement by the athlete in that sport, *while providing an overall high-quality experience*, including strong, positive connections with all athletes, a positive, respectful, fun, non-threatening, success-oriented working environment, and an attitude that values the athlete as a respected person—not just as an athlete.

Incidentally, if a coach truly views their athletes as valued people (whether they be age seven or seventeen) and not as numbers or pieces of some grand scheme, then he or she will allow the athletes to be (and act) their age. A thirteen- year-old boy has certain idiosyncrasies, as does an eight- year-old girl. Don't demand that they be little adults, with all the attendant impossible expectations. Of course all your athletes, of any age, should behave with politeness and respect. Certainly teach and encourage them to behave in the highest quality fashion—any time. But thirteen-year-olds will act like thirteen-year-olds sometimes—that's what they are! Be okay with it and try hard to understand. It is a basic form of coach/athlete respect that should not be underestimated.

The Mind Must Be Open to Receive

This tenet seems obvious. It is absolutely crucial to the transmission of information, yet is often overlooked. We assume our athletes are listening to us, yet are they? Sometimes, no. And even if they are listening, are they really hearing the message? Are they taking in what you want them to? Most important, are they picking up your message clearly enough and with enough interest that they *retain* what you just said? You have the knowledge, you transmitted it, but was it received, and to what degree? Chances are that if the athlete is talking to someone else, or if his or her mind is on something else, or if the subject, or the way it is being presented, is uninteresting, your message is lost. To make sure we are communicating effectively (i.e. both sending and receiving), we must recognize when athletes are not listening, develop specific attention-getting and retaining techniques, and develop a positive, learning and growth-promoting environment in which your athletes really want to learn and improve. Let's start with that all-important learning environment.

Creating a Mind-Opening Learning Environment

Communicating effectively with your athletes starts with the creation of an environment that helps athletes *want* to learn and succeed, and that allows them the freedom to fail without feeling a failure. Such an environment is respectful, supportive, positive, challenging, and focused on improvement. Here are some suggestions on how to create such an environment:

1. **Make it Fun:** Fun often means different things to different age groups, but if one of your athletes remark how much fun that practice was, you're usually on the right track. By "fun" I'm not referring to whether the practice is easy physically or more difficult. Rather, fun is when an athlete of any age says "I'm into it," which means the athlete's senses are fully engaged in the activity. For younger age group athletes, the weaving of stories, games, and other imaginative devices into your practices sparks their interest and excitement, while older athletes will appreciate your creating

new and different ways to drill and challenge them. Bottom line—creating a setting where it is fun to practice will go a long way toward your athletes being more fully engaged in your sport and more open to your guidance.

2. **Build a Culture of Success:** Creating a culture where the dominant theme is improvement (not the status quo) and the goal is excellence fosters intellectual and sensory engagement. It is a motivating milieu. Athletes are fully engaged in becoming better at their sport. As well, practices tend to be more stimulating, interesting, and fun *because* there is such a strong, united focus on attaining excellence. Contrast an invigorating, excellence-oriented practice session with a workout where there are no goals or focus and you will begin to imagine the difference in energy level and attentiveness between the two.

3. **Create Opportunities for Success:** The younger the athlete, the more they thrive on success and have difficulty with failure. Success might be mastering a simple drill, or going faster for a particular distance than before. Create practices that are challenging, yet ultimately do-able for all concerned. Make sure your athletes leave practice with a feeling of accomplishment and success. Create challenges within practice sessions that are athlete-specific, such as breaking their own push-up record. Being more mature emotionally, older athletes handle failures better. Yet they, too, become more motivated through succeeding.

4. **Free to Fail:** To grow up well rounded, youngsters need to learn how to handle failures big and small. To do this, they need to experience failures successfully. Learning a sport in a positive, supportive environment gives the child a great opportunity to do this. You create such an environment by not yelling at or putting down athletes who make mistakes, by addressing such mistakes as learning opportunities, and by addressing and correcting the action, not denigrating the person. Eventually, an athlete operating in dread of failing stops listening or even trying. Conversely, a lack of fear opens the mind and body to all possibilities.

The All-Important C-A Connection

Establishing a strong, respectful Coach-Athlete connection with all your charges should be a top priority. It shouldn't be hard to do for most coaches, new or otherwise, because most find that they *like* working with age group athletes. In any event, make this a top priority. Otherwise, your upside as an effective coach will be limited, since the C-A connection is as important as any of the above learning-environment suggestions for opening the mind to instruction and guidance. But how does one build a strong C-A connection? Basically by showing you genuinely *care* about them in all ways:

- Pay some attention to each athlete every day. Say hi, comment on their form, ask them about school, correct them, praise them. That's a few interactions right there. Oftentimes you will connect more, depending on the flow of the practice or contest that day. The key is to be consistent. Connect at least sometime every day with each athlete.

- Get to know their names, and quickly. "Wow, Coach already knows my name and it's only the second day of practice!" I hear this kind of thing often from parents giving me initial feedback on how things are going. A seemingly small thing like swiftly learning a child's name can have such an impact. Taking attendance every day, playing name games with them (younger athletes), attaching performance to names (in rowing, for example, knowing your athletes' best ergo meter times helps connect time to name, thus making it easier to remember names), are all great methods of committing name to memory.

- Listen to Them. They should feel that their opinion is valuable, that they are worthy of being listened to and not merely ordered around. All athletes, no matter the age, should feel that what they have to say bears attention and merit. Another form of respect.

- Get to Know Them Better. Several years ago I had an incorrigible bully in my nine-to-eleven-year-old swim stroke technique class. He wouldn't listen, didn't seem to care at all about learning, and constantly caused fusses in his lane. One day we happened to be alone before class began and I asked him, quite innocuously, what he liked to do if it wasn't swimming. What proceeded was a lengthy response about Star Wars and space ships and the latest alien movie he had just been to, a conversation that regrettably had to be cut off so class could begin. Do you know he never gave me trouble again? Of course, not all situations will be resolved so neatly and positively just because you get to know an athlete better. But your caring, and the showing of it, moves relationships in a positive direction. This young man had come to realize that he wasn't just a number, that someone had taken an interest in him, not just in his ability to do that sport.

- Be Respectful at All Times (even when joking around). No sarcasm, no putdowns. Look them in the eye. Be sincere. No matter what their age.

- Make Them Feel Important. Ask your athletes, younger or older, to help set up practice equipment. They jump at it. At times ask their advice, whether or not you act on it. Let your athletes know when they did something that helped the team or was important in other respects. Announce to the whole group how great was so-and-so's contribution. That's not playing favorites, because *all* your athletes know you are proud of all of them (if you simply apply the preceding suggestions to each of your athletes), because you've made it a habit to acknowledge *all* your athletes when it is deserved.

You have reached the highest level C-A connection when each of your athletes thinks they are special to you. Not merely important—special. When you've reached this level, your athletes don't worry about favoritism because, in a way, they all think they are your favorite. Accusations of mistreatment or better treatment become rare because *all* are cared for and looked after exceptionally well.

Note: The C-A connection isn't about the coach being friends or buddies with the athletes, and it's certainly not about us acting or operating at their level. It is about an older, more mature person caring deeply for the child while desiring to help each of them progress in that sport. By making a strong connection, you become more effective as a coach (again, you can be effective without such a connection, but not *as* effective). The more you care about them, the more they will care about what you are doing, the more they will listen, try, and try to please you, resulting in a better quality of learning in terms of clarity, staying power, persistence, and performance.

Specific Techniques for Opening the Mind

Creating a supportive, caring, mind-opening learning environment is part of the solution. What words or actions can we use to most effectively hold their attention throughout the countless daily interactions? Surely someone will be daydreaming during one of your explanations, or thinking of their boy- or girlfriend during practice instructions, or temporarily resentful or disappointed (and distracted) after a sub-par performance. And don't be fooled! I've witnessed team talks and lectures where all the athletes were silent, yet few were actually listening (vacant eyes, fiddling with equipment, grinning at their friend) as the coach droned on. So what specific techniques can we use to gain or regain their attention to ensure that information is both received and retained? Here are some suggestions:

1. **Look Them in the Eye:** They will see you are intent on *them*, and will tend to respond with more focus and attention. As well, you will be able to "read" them instantly and know if they are with you or not.

2. **Offer an Honest Compliment:** Who doesn't want to hear themselves praised for something well done? Using a compliment as, say, an opening line before a discussion of an athlete's performance, is a great technique for immediately getting them to focus in on what's being said. The "compliment sandwich" is one example of using praise to begin an interaction successfully.

3. **Be Enthusiastic:** It is infectious, contagious. Certainly the opposite of putting someone to sleep!

4. **Tell a Good Story:** All ages will hang on every word of a well-told, interesting tale, whether fiction or fact. Your story may have a sport-specific purpose or be pulled out of thin air, but it's a great way to begin a practice, discussion, or set of instructions. One super technique when coaching the very young is to purposely mess up the details of a tale they may already know. They *love* pouncing on your mistakes and correcting you. You sure do get their attention!

5. **Be a Good Listener:** What interests them? What is their take on the situation? Ask their read on things and they will be more inclined to hear yours.

You should always know whether your athletes are paying attention (when you ask it of them). These techniques not only provide methods for gaining their attention, but also ways for monitoring whether they are focused on your message. Moreover, you should care that they are (or aren't) listening to you. That speaks to your own desire to be great at what you do.

Yes, you are the coach, so they should listen to you—automatically! But that doesn't mean they do, for various reasons. These basic communication techniques should help, as will many others we examine later, to directly or indirectly help the athlete focus more intently on instructions, suggestions, commands, and the action that occurs in your practices and contests.

Preparation Before the Practice or Contest

You can almost guarantee that a practice will accomplish a fair amount, or that you will handle a competition professionally, if you prepare and rehearse ahead of time what you will say and do. Below are the basic steps that, when executed, will help you become more prepared and confident going into that activity.

1. **Know Your Subject:** Seems obvious, but must be included in our discussion of the steps coaches should take toward giving the best lesson possible that day. In general, the more you know your subject, the more confident you will be, and the more professional your delivery will tend to be. Supplement the knowledge you've acquired from such sources as fellow coaches, clinics, books, magazines, and online information. In addition, if it's critical for team success, before a contest learn all you can about the opposition and what you can do to have a better chance against them. In any event, as head coach you will be the expert your athletes and assistant coaches look to for answers. If you don't know an answer, 'fess up. Be honest, say you don't know, and vow to find the answer or direct the athlete to a source that can help.

2. **Never Stop Learning, and make it one of your success Attitudes:** We don't know it all. What's more, lessons grow stale and athletes become bored when hearing the same stuff, delivered the same way, time after time. Constantly be on the hunt for new ways of thinking about and teaching your sport. Keep up with the latest ideas. Find new ways of getting across what you know. Borrow or create new drills. Keep it fresh! Constantly challenging yourself to know more and finding better ways to get across what you know are among the hallmarks of a great coach.

3. **Plan Ahead:** This seems obvious, but make sure you have a fairly clear idea of what you want to accomplish and how you are going to go about it before that day's action. First think it through, then review or rehearse the important details. I often think about my practices while jogging. I'll flesh out the objectives, then go over and over the order in which I want things to go, as well as the words and emphases I will use. This repeated mental rehearsal has two huge benefits. First, aspects of the practice that may not be working can be thrown out and replaced with more effective steps.

Second, by visualizing each step all the way through to a successful conclusion, you gain confidence that the practice will indeed succeed to the level you expect. Rehearse the words you will use in your speeches as well, like an actor. I guarantee this technique makes one far more assured in both delivery and emphasis.

4. **Write it Down:** There are good reasons that college teaching courses emphasize and teach how to create detailed, written lesson plans: When creating and writing a lesson plan, we learn how to think through the details of what we want to accomplish, clarify the order in which aspects of a practice will be run, and emphasize items of importance. And because we wrote it down, we have notes to refer to, should we need them.

However (there's always a "however"), be flexible! Especially when coaching the younger age grouper, sticking religiously to "the plan" is often a recipe for failure. Why? Several reasons. Since generally children this age are not yet dedicated to their sport, their main motivation for being there is fun. Therefore, you will often need to change a drill or activity just to keep them engaged. Another reason: Youngsters' attention and excitement often occur in surges or bursts, after which they are either spent or their attention has wandered. In other words, their surges of energy and attention often stray from your written script for the day! Consider as well that, especially with athletes newer to the sport, you may have assigned a certain amount of time to the acquisition of a skill, but they may struggle with it longer than you planned. You may therefore decide to work longer on the skill so that they may experience success, instead of stopping while they are still scratching their heads. Decisions like these are often made at that moment, based on your skillful reassessment of what would be best for your particular athletes.

The result of such preparation will be a more effectively run session—guaranteed. Skill acquisition, drills, and training will all have more meaning and flow more smoothly. In addition, you will be more sure of yourself, more confident. That aura of command is infectious. You *know* what you want to accomplish and how, and your athletes sense that and respond positively.

During The Practice or Contest: How to Treat Your Athletes

How *should* coaches treat their athletes? The simple answer is, with respect. Follow this one simple suggestion, and you will never be too far off base. Let's flesh out just what "with respect" means:

1. **As Valued Team Members.** As a coach, if you believe all your athletes are important one way or another (as people, as well as valuable team members), you *will* treat each one with respect. They each bring a unique combination of personality and abilities to your team. So don't rank as to who is more valuable. Keep it simple and respectful by treating all the same, as valued members.

2. **As Age-Invisible as Possible.** I treat my seven-year-olds the same as the seventeen-year olds when it comes to basic human politeness and decency. "Please" and "thank you" works superbly, no matter the age. Moreover, most any respectful words or actions will be appreciated by any age group. People ask me "why make such a big deal over this?" Two reasons: You are establishing the value of each individual to the team, and you as coach are building a powerfully positive connection with each of your athletes. It starts the day an athlete joins your group. It is unbelievable how positively your athlete (especially the very young) will respond to your consistently respectful actions over time. You may not notice at first, but eventually the sheer accumulation of respectful actions shown toward him or her will result in your athlete responding more positively to you and your coaching than you can imagine.

3. **With Honesty and Sincerity.** Beyond the fact that it is the right way to behave, dealing always honestly with your athletes helps build their trust in you, leading to a higher quality C-A relationship. For instance, admitting you don't know an answer is crucial when establishing trust and building respect. In addition, telling falsehoods to your athletes will generally hamper their development. For instance, your athletes trust you to observe them as dispassionately, rationally, and truthfully as possible. If you tell them they are performing correctly when something really is wrong with their technique, they will perform poorly and not understand why. Honest communication, a key to great coaching, will have been com-

promised. Your athletes, above all else, need to know how they truly are performing.

4. **Without Embarrassing Them.** To a teenager, nothing is worse than being ridiculed or made fun of in front of peers. To younger age groupers, embarrassment in front of the group can quite simply shatter what little confidence they have. This is a bigger deal than we adults and coaches sometimes recognize. We can find amusement and enjoyment in our sport without being sarcastic to our athletes or pinning (sometimes) hateful nicknames on them. We are their allies, their advocates. We build them up—at least that's what we should do.

5. **Create Realistic Expectations Based on Age and Developmental Levels.** In other words, recognize and be okay with the fact that children and teenagers will generally act like children and teenagers, not men and women. Treat them as age-invisible as possible, but expect and be fine with them acting their age and performing at their developmental level.

6. **Confine Criticism to Their Actions.** It's timeout, late in the fourth quarter of a tight basketball game. In one huddle the coach is blasting the center for "tripping over his big feet" and "being stupid" while "allowing" the opposing center to make three quick scores. Meanwhile, in the other huddle, the coach points out to his two forwards how to better position themselves when on defense, then designs the next play. It is so much more positive and effective to focus on the game, not point fingers and get personal.

7. **Listen, Don't Just Command.** This goes for all age groups. Your athletes will have questions and opinions. Hear them out, just like you would any adult. To them, your patiently, intently listening to what they have to say means a lot.

Methods of Communication

You are prepared. You've created a plan, a blueprint for what you want to accomplish that day. How do you implement it? How do you communicate the plan effectively, such that your athletes understand and respond to your instructions?

Verbal Communication

1. **Be Clear.** Instructions should be simple while still being complete. Don't jazz up explanations with needless detail. Be straightforward and to the point. We are trying to be effective, not win a speech award.

2. **Use Vocabulary That Is Understood by Your Age Group.** This involves familiarizing yourself with the level of vocabulary your charges possess. Just as important, learn to read the signs as to whether your athletes got what you said. Ask them if they got it (if you aren't sure), and, of course, rephrase your instructions in simpler terms if they give you that blank look.

3. **The use of Distinctive Names, Phrases, or Examples .** One's choice of whether and when to use this technique depends partly on your own personality and style. Younger children especially tend to remember procedures and/or instructions better when they equate those instructions with unusual, funny, or otherwise distinctive phrases or characters. "Be Willie Mays" might mean holding the baseball bat a certain way. "Make an arrow" may refer to a swimmer's desirable body position when diving in or pushing off. "Instant replay" might refer to an athlete's incredible play, and so on. Any unusual name or phrase that resonates with the athletes you are teaching can act as an effective memory trigger.

4. **Be Positive, Encouraging, Enthusiastic.** In other words, use the volume and tone of your voice to project your passion for your sport and for them.

5. **Project, Don't Shout.** Be loud enough only to be heard clearly. Do not allow anger or negativism into the tone of your voice. Naturally, we have to raise our voices occasionally due to acoustics, distance from the athletes, and so on. When you do raise your voice, make sure to project, not shout or yell. *Projecting* is when a coach's vocal emissions are louder, but controlled, neutral or positive (non-angry), and instructive. *Yelling* or *shouting* implies some anger or lack of control. Neither is as effective or respectful as when one projects.

6. **Vary Your Volume to Gain Attention and Focus.** One of the most effective techniques I know for gaining a group's attention is to speak more softly than you had been. Heads automatically lean in to hear what's going on. Athletes will demand to hear what they

missed. You will have their attention. Also, varying the volume when explaining, suggesting, instructing, etc., comes across as more interesting than when speaking in a monotone.

7. **Use your bully pulpit!** Fill their heads with encouragement, with motivational tales, with moral teachings, with praise for their great efforts, and with visions of what they can become! Get across your philosophy of success! You have a captive audience! Imagine what positive things you can say to them! All based on truth of course, on knowledge and experience you have had, as well as on the skills, capabilities, and energies they have exhibited. Think of this technique as feeding them *highly nutritious verbal food.* Positive stuff; encouragement, constructive criticism, observations, praise. What a golden opportunity to motivate, to build up! Young age groupers respond incredibly well to such attentions, but this applies to all age group athletes, not just the younger ones. Some coaches feel the high school athlete is beyond this sort of thing , that taking a few minutes out of a practice to verbally motivate or just discuss what's on their minds is precious time taken away from training. I strongly believe that those few (or more) minutes can be the most important parts of any practice, whether they are all at once or scattered about throughout a practice session. The practice will run better, the athletes will get more out of the practice time, motivation will increase, and your athletes will feel you care more for their overall well-being (which helps grease all wheels), if you take some time each day to talk to, encourage, and listen to them.

Non-Verbal Communication

1. **Modeling.** Ideally your gestures, facial features, and overall body language will convey a sense of enthusiasm, caring, and can-do action. Recognize that your appearance and actions have an impact on your charges and that you want your body language to be consistent with the messages you are trying to send. It is counterproductive (rude and juvenile as well) to preach openness and caring, then look bored or turn your back and walk away from an athlete who is talking to you. I have heard coaches admonish their athletes to "get excited," then go sit in a chair. Another example: Athletes will take their cue from you in the heat of a contest. They will watch your face and notice your reactions to referees' calls. What

does it tell them when you counsel "obey the refs," then they see you throw down your glasses, stamp on the ground, then yell at the official for a call that didn't go your team's way! It's what you do, not just what you say, that has an impact.

2. **Smile!** The single biggest lifter of spirits is a simple smile. It's the best way to show optimism and a sense of positivism. Who doesn't want to be around such a leader?

3. **Handshake, High Five, Pat on the Back.** Virtually all research shows that physical contact—touch—is beneficial for both body and soul. Yet due to worries about the very few who have been inappropriate or sexually abusive, the use of touch, when teaching or coaching children, has been for years frowned upon. *Any* touching. Fact is, there are certain kinds of contact that are wonderful for calming, reassuring, uniting, motivating, and that are far from even a hint of inappropriateness. I could hug whoever first threw a "high-five." That gesture, the slapping of palms above the head, is a great way to get across congratulations, as well as a feeling of kinship, of unity, of shared excitement. Bumping elbows and other similar actions serve similar purposes. Volleyball players often clasp hands or put their arms around each other's shoulders to convey solidarity and team spirit, a great example of how touch bonds and unites.

   Placing a hand on a disappointed athlete's shoulder to comfort and show you care is an example of how touch can have a powerful positive effect. Here is an example: When I am talking to a parent or athlete and a second athlete rushes up, needing attention, I will (often without looking) place my hand on that second athlete's shoulder while finishing the conversation with the first person— signaling that I know he or she is there, is important, and will be tended to in just a minute. No one feels rejected. (Note: be aware that some of your athletes may shy away from any physical contact. Respect their feelings.) Then there is the good old handshake, now seemingly almost a lost art. However, for the showing of respect and appreciation, there isn't another gesture that comes close. The firm handshake while looking directly into another person's eyes is a surefire way to express sincere congratulations and show honest appreciation for a job well done. From any age to any age, the handshake is a universal sign of respect.

4. **Physically Guiding Their Actions** Sometimes younger age groupers will be unable to perform a skill, even after witnessing a demonstration. When teaching how to hold a football, actually place the child's fingers in the proper place. When teaching the butterfly pull, actually hold the swimmer's wrists as you mimic the motion. Physically guiding your athletes' motions can often help them make the connection that eludes them when just seeing or hearing instructions.

Feedback

Whether it is a recounting of their performance in a contest or the active give-and-take that goes on in a practice, athletes want to know (and should be told) how they are doing. Your feedback to them will generally take the form of praise, criticism, neutral observation, or a combination thereof.

1. **Praise.** In the chapter on motivation, we touched on the importance of praise as a motivating force. Earlier in this chapter we recognized the act of praising as an effective mind-opening technique. Let us add a third critical use for praise—as a guidepost to show the athlete how he or she is performing. Truthful compliments are a sure way for athletes to know they are on the right track, but the key is to be truthful.

2. **Neutral, Impartial Performance Reviews.** When athletes check in with their coaches after a performance or during a game, a good deal of the feedback involves a dispassionate recounting of what the coach saw, as opposed to an opinion. During a practice, much of what passes back and forth are neutral observations as well. A football coach telling the quarterback that he dropped back seven steps instead of eight, a swim coach barking out times during a set, or a soccer coach reminding the team that there are only forty seconds left in the game or scrimmage are all important pieces of information, and neutral (neither compliment or criticism).

3. **Constructive Criticism.** Certainly equal to praise in importance as an accurate appraisal of how the athlete performed is the constructive critique. Make no mistake, to do best by your athletes, they need to know when they are not doing something right. The art is in *how* you go about such a critique. Some suggestions:

   • Never criticize without providing a solution as well.

   • Criticize the actions, not the person.

- Know when enough is enough. Particularly younger or novice athletes can only take so much, regardless of how well you frame the constructive critique. They can become defeated, even temporarily quit on you. If you see those kinds of signs, lay off for awhile, or try another way of getting your message across.

- Criticize with a neutral voice. In other words, don't allow anger, frustration, or other negative emotions to be heard. This can be a challenge sometimes, but the rewards for being dispassionate, though perhaps not immediately noticed, are numerous.

- Teach your charges that mistakes and errors are actually opportunities to find out what doesn't work; therefore, constructive criticism is a *good thing*, a way to help them learn. Especially for the very young, once they understand the positive nature of constructive criticism (and that their coach isn't mad at them, that in fact he or she is trying to help them), they tend to "break out," i.e. start learning much more quickly and with more fervor.

Other Forms of Communication

1. **Film and Videotape.** A picture is worth a thousand words. Put another way, one learns faster and retains far more, the more vivid the lesson. For example, say you are a student sitting in a geography class. The teacher is lecturing about Venice, Italy. You hear about the architecture, the canals, the history. You get some idea of the uniqueness of such a place. Then the teacher shows you pictures of Venice. Now you have a more exact, more vivid impression. "So that's what Venice looks like!" you say. An even higher quality of learning and retention can be attained by watching a movie about the city, actually observing the boats traveling the canals, people walking in the piazzas and taking in all the sights and sounds of this amazing place. However, the most vivid impressions and memories of this or any place will occur if one actually visits or lives there. The sights, sounds, smells, the energy, and the atmosphere are all around you. People tend to learn more thoroughly and remember more clearly and for much longer the closer one gets to the real thing. Same in the coaching/athletic arena. Most of our teaching will be done verbally—instructions, commands, and explanations. But often athletes need a clearer picture of how to perform this or that skill, play, or drill. Film, videotape, and demonstrations are all ways

to more vividly illustrate the right way to perform, and in conjunction with a coach's play by play, help athletes learn more speedily and retain what they learned for far longer.

- **Show"How-to" Films.** Whether you show movies of great athletes playing the sport at the highest level, or "How to" DVDs teaching the elements of your sport, movies and videos are tremendous for athletes, both educationally and motivationally. Realistically, older aged athletes whose programs have the time for occasional film sessions can make excellent use of this educational method, while younger age group programs generally won't be allotted enough time in their practice schedules for movie watching. Yet even with the younger athletes, making time once in a while to watch such a movie can add variety and an added dimension to their overall sport-awareness. You can rent or buy the appropriate films through your sport's governing organization or other similar organizations.

- **Videotaping.** Athletes have some idea how they look and how their bodies are actually moving, but they don't know as precisely as if they could actually see themselves in action. Watching themselves adds that extra dimension of seeing, as well as feeling, how they are performing. Athletes sometimes will see areas to improve when before they thought no improvement was needed. To see film of oneself is an awareness-expanding experience and especially older age group athletes will greatly benefit from being videotaped, then either watching it with their coach or by having things set up so that the athlete can come in on his or her own and view tape. Younger age groupers may enjoy seeing themselves on tape, but their relative (to older athletes) lack of kinesthetic awareness makes this technique less effective for them.

2. **Demonstrations.** During a practice there will often be times when a well- executed demonstration of what is being taught will get the message across more quickly and clearly than an explanation. Most of the time, you will do the demonstrating. The key to any effective demonstration is that it be performed correctly, as you are augmenting your verbal instructions with a visual of how the skill should be performed. If you aren't moving your body correctly, how will they get the desired message? Practice in front of a mirror if you have to, to make sure the images you are projecting are the ones you want your athletes to receive.

For several reasons you may elect to have one of your fellow coaches or athletes perform the demonstration:

- The person you pick may be able to perform the demonstration better than you can.
- The setting may not be conducive to your doing the demo yourself. Coaches of water sports have this issue often. Either it takes too much time out of practice to disrobe, hop in, demo, then hop out and dry off (when an athlete could perform the demo in a fraction of the time), or, for safety reasons, the coach has to remain on deck, overseeing the group. Of course your demonstrating could be quite a good motivational move ("Coach is getting in. I want to see this!"), in which case you may plan to demonstrate even though it does take extra practice time.

  You may want to narrate the action while another person demonstrates, also a powerfully effective use of this technique. Most athletes love demonstrating in front of their peers. Giving them a chance once in awhile is motivational, educational, and another way to add variety and spike interest.

- You may want to motivate one of your athletes by calling him or her in front of the group to show the correct way to do something. I do this all the time with my younger swimmers. On a certain day, I may see a certain athlete in need of a little confidence or recognition boost. If that person can perform the skill correctly, I'll ask him or her to step up and show how it should be done. The group sees it done right, the athlete feels good about his or her contribution. Two birds with one stone.

  Demonstrations build variety into practices and aid motivation as well. But their primary function (and effectiveness as a teaching technique) is to *instantly and vividly show* the correct way to perform a skill. Again, a picture is worth a thousand words. I have often noticed an instant improvement with my group after a well-performed demonstration.

Discipline

To many, the word *discipline* is synonymous with penalty or punishment. For our purposes, discipline means a state of order and the obeying of rules. Especially with younger athletes who are less capable of controlling themselves, how do we establish a disciplined, orderly status to our practices and contests? And how should we deal with situations where athletes deviate too far from the overall team's productive state?

A Sense of Discipline

Perhaps the biggest challenge a coach of elementary school-aged athletes faces is that of welding together a bunch of energetic youngsters(who just want to play) into a unit that works together. Certainly one of the secrets of successfully coaching this very youngest of age groups is to keep things fun while the athletes learn and improve. But central to any kind of group improvement, regardless of age, is that the athletes need to be able to follow instructions from those in charge while working together as a group. These concepts are quite new to most five- and six-year-olds, and to some seven- to ten-year- olds as well, and tend to be difficult for them to follow. To begin the discipline process, sit them down on the very first day of practice and explain why following a system, maintaining order, and obeying instructions and rules will give them a chance to improve while having fun at the same time. Remind them that improvement *is* fun and that they can become better at that sport, individually and as a group, by following directions and working with each other.

During that first meeting with any age group team, make them aware of any basic rules you want them to follow. Further, help them understand *why* each rule exists (for safety, to increase productivity, etc.) when you explain rules and consequences. The more they understand why, the more they will tend to go along, and the more they will feel respected, regardless of whether they agree with the rules. Yes, even the youngest athletes will sense that you care about their welfare and are respecting them when you take these extra steps.

During the practices that follow, praise and support improvement in their ability to follow commands and work cohesively. Compliment your athletes just as much for following instructions as for performing a skill correctly. They are in the early process of learning how to be a disciplined athlete, which is as much an acquired skill as kicking a ball.

Preventing Discipline Issues From Occurring

At times athletes may deviate too much from acceptable behavior. Often all it will take to bring errant athletes back into line is a whistle or command. Should an athlete commit a more serious infraction, or ignore your warnings to shape up in the first place, you should implement a plan of action that is well thought out in advance. However, your most effective disciplinary "weapon," if you will, isn't a punishment at all. Fact: The more engaged your athletes are in what they are doing, the fewer discipline problems occur.

In my experience, the vast majority of potential discipline issues don't even have a chance of getting started if the group is fully engaged in the practice or contest. Therefore, focus on making practices and contests fun, interesting, even exciting, so that your charges are totally into what is going on. Put extra effort into planning the workout so that action and involvement are virtually continuous, except for scripted breaks. For younger athletes, it is the standing in line for long periods and the boredom caused by inaction that breed "questionable alternative types of entertainment" such as pushing and shoving, name-calling, yelling and screaming at inappropriate times, and worse.

· ·

A Coach's Plan for Discipline

The following is a "flow chart," a plan of action in chronological order. Notice that the first two are preventive measures and that prevention is a far better solution than having to punish after the fact.

Preventive Measures

Keep Your Athletes Engaged. Ideally, your athletes should always have something to do: planning, stretching, visualizing, or otherwise preparing to act. Idle minds (and hands and feet) are the bane of order and an invitation to chaos!

Make Sure Your Athletes Know and Understand the Rules. In general, the fewer rules the better. Don't make a rule unless it is necessary. Each rule should have a valid basis and clearly understood consequences. Make sure you spell out the rules right at the outset of your season, as well as why that rule exists. That way everyone knows the parameters from the very beginning. It is the fairest and the best way to ensure smooth, productive workouts and contests from day one.

Disciplinary Measures

1. Disciplinary Step 1: Take the Athlete Aside, Away from Peers. Talk to them in a quiet but serious way. Find out why they were acting out and explain why their behavior was unacceptable and cannot continue; also, remind them of the correct behavior. Dealing with the athlete away from his or her peers is a more respectful way to handle the situation, as it reduces unwanted attention and potential embarrassment to the athlete. As well, you and the athlete can more fully concentrate on the issue and the solution. This method works well with all ages of athletes.

2. Disciplinary Step 2: A Pause, Break, Cool Down, or Timeout. For whatever reasons, an athlete sometimes loses self-control, even after you have taken them aside and talked to them about their transgression. Especially for younger athletes, a reasonable next step is to take them away from the action and sit them down for a short period. This removal, theoretically at least, from what they want to be doing often gets them refocused on behaving the right way. It usually settles them down some, and often all they need is a bit of rest and recuperation. Take this time to remind them, if necessary, that it's a privilege to be involved with the team and that their actions will decide if this privilege should be taken away, temporarily or otherwise. Though you probably wouldn't use a "timeout" approach with high school athletes, keeping them from the activity until you're satisfied with their commitment would be in order. Again, focus on correcting the behavior, short and long term, not just on punishing the athlete.

3. Disciplinary Step 3: Talk with the Athlete's Parents. It's unfortunate when a situation gets this far, but if, despite your repeated attempts to resolve an issue, the behavior persists and the athlete continues to negatively affect the group, a chat with mom or dad may be necessary. Behavior has to change. Can the parents shed some light on what's going on? What I have found most valuable in these talks is that I often get a better perspective of the athlete's motivations. Why is this athlete participating in your program? For instance, if the child loves the sport but has anger management issues, one would handle the situation far differently than, say, if the child hated the sport but was being forced to participate.

These talks should not be viewed merely as you bearing bad news. Quite the opposite. You are finding out background that will help solve the problem as well as help you coach the athlete better. In addition, talking with parents will likely gain you a valuable ally, as the parent will see that you care about helping their child, and they will tend to work with you to help solve whatever issue exists.

Note: As your athletes grow older, calling parents should

become more and more a last resort, partly because the teenager has more control over him-or herself, physically, emotionally, mentally, and decision making-wise. Calls are also less warranted with this age group because beyond the age of twelve or thirteen most athletes usually have taken some form of ownership for their sport and efforts involved in it.

▶ Summary Points ▶ ▶ ▶

▶ A coach's main objective is to help the athlete grow, in the sport and in life, while providing as high-quality an experience as possible.

▶ Athletes' minds must be open and ready to take in the messages you send. Techniques for creating a mind-opening environment include making team participation fun, building a culture and history of success, and by building strong C-A (coach-athlete) connections.

▶ Guarantee the professional operation of practices and contests by: knowing your subject, planning and rehearsing speeches and practice flow, and writing down your lesson plans.

▶ Treat your athletes always as valued team members, as age-invisible as possible, without embarrassing them, and always with respect, honesty, and sincerity.

▶ Methods of communication include verbal (use clear, positive, age-appropriate words); non-verbal (modeling, facial features, hand-shakes and high-fives); feedback (praise, impartial review, constructive criticism); and other forms (films, videotapes, and demonstrations).

▶ Your rules and and expectations need to be shared with your athletes to ensure that practices and contests are run in a disciplined, orderly fashion. Coaches must do their best to run these activities in a way that will keep athletes as fully engaged as possible.

6

Parents: A Coach's Most Valuable Allies

Before we get into our discussion about the important role parents play in your organization, allow me first to pose this question to all parents: In a perfect world, what kind of person would you want your child to be by the time he or she is entering adulthood? If I'm not missing my guess, you would generally hope that your children are:

- happy, self-motivated, and well-adjusted.
- hard workers, accomplishing a great deal and finding much of it rewarding.
- good at some things and passionate about a few.
- knowledgeable about themselves, including their strengths and weaknesses.
- socially adept and comfortable.
- compassionate and loving people.

In other words, without necessarily being the absolute best at any one thing, your children, you would hope, are really something and quite a success.

All of that may seem a bit fanciful, yet it is realistic. And although parents are by far the most responsible for their children's achieving these most reachable ideals, there are key players who can positively assist them in the process. These include, among others, family, teachers, religious leaders, significant peers, and, of course, coaches.

Now it might seem obvious that these key players, having shared interests, would want to work together with parents to better serve the children. Unfortunately, some coaches feel uncomfortable getting close to parents or even getting to know them on a basic level, as if the parent might end up intruding too much on the coach's "territory." As a result, parents sometimes feel shut out. At the same time, parents do recognize the sacrifice of time and effort a coach makes and fear being overly intrusive. For these and other reasons, the critical connection between coach and parent may not occur. In this chapter, we aim to suggest ways that can alter the exclusionary mindset of many coaches and help parents and coaches come together, because a healthy, positive parent-coach relationship can only benefit the child.

In this chapter we will discuss the Foundation Attitudes inherent in successful parent-coach relationships, contrast and compare the role of the coach with that of the parent, and detail the characteristics and behavior of supportive parents. We will also include guidelines a coach can use when suggesting to parents how to get the most out of the time spent watching their son or daughter during practices and contests, as well as categorizing the many ways parents can help the coach and the team. However, we will begin with a discussion of the Foundation Attitudes that foster respect and unity of purpose between coach and parent. The Foundation Attitudes are based on the "big picture," that is, the development of the athlete in life. Understanding these attitudes should help both parent and coach keep that wonderful, realistic "big picture" ideal in mind at all times, ensuring that short-term actions and decisions affecting the athlete will occur more often in the right way and for the right reasons.

A Coach's Foundation Attitude Toward Parents

Because they are the mothers and fathers of your athletes, team parents are significant team members as well. Yes, their role may be more behind the scenes, but it's still integral to the success of the team. (After all, if the car pool doesn't get to practice, no improvement occurs.) Parents organize meets, fundraisers, and other functions that support the team. Also, parents are uniquely knowledgeable about their child's intellectual, emotional, and social makeup. For instance, they can tell you whether their son or daughter is physically challenged in some way, or has a learning disability and, therefore, can advise you as to which methods of instruction have been most effective under certain circumstances. Parents are key assets to your program, and a savvy coach will tap into this valuable source of knowledge. Though coaches generally spend only a small fraction of their overall coaching time communicating with parents, it is vital that you, the coach, initiate and foster a positive, vibrant relationship with your athletes' parents.

A coach's appreciation of the major role parents play in the success of the team will strengthen the parent-coach relationship. A second factor that can only enhance relations is if the coach always keeps the big picture in mind with regard to the athlete. In other words, sport is not an end in itself, but rather a means to the greater end of personal development. Parents often encourage their son or daughter to participate in a sport because improvement and success in that sport develops success attitudes and skills that will help the child succeed in life. By embracing the High Quality Method of coaching (discussed in Chapter 5), we will be supporting that big-picture view as well.

This two-part Foundation Attitude grounds the relationship between the coach and the parents by means of a mutual acknowledgement that (1) the parent is an invaluable member of the team (and great source of information about the child) and that (2) the coach's dual objective is to help their child succeed in both the sport and in the bigger arena of life. Establishing this attitude from the start will help trust and communication grow, resulting in the whole team operating more effectively and the athletes having a more fulfilling experience.

Parents' Foundation Attitudes

Support and Facilitate a Child's Participation, but Let It Be the Child's "Thing"

Of course a parent wants the best for his or her child. Of course! But what *is* best? Is it what the parent thinks is best? Usually, it is, because parents know their children so well. Parents will tend to sign up their offspring for activities in which the child either shows some talent or a desire to participate. There can be other valid, big-picture reasons why parents enroll their children. For instance, parents moving to a new community may sign up their child for the local Little League team chiefly to meet new friends and develop a sense of belonging.

However, what happens when a parent confuses what's best for Mary with what Mom or Dad wants Mary to become? Frequently, parents transfer their own viewpoint or wants onto the child. The results are often similar to the myopia that occurs when a coach gets too wrapped up in short-term gain to the exclusion of long-term development. For instance, a father who is a doctor thinks his son should be one, too, despite the fact that his son loves music, is quite talented, and can't stand the sight of blood. Or a mother who was an aspiring skater till she blew out her knee sees similar talent in her daughter. Rather than facilitating and allowing her daughter to evolve naturally, she throws all her energy into realizing her daughter's (whose?) dreams. Result? Quite possibly negative. A parent's transference of his or her own dreams onto the child (if the child is not equally as zealous) can lead to burnout and/or rebellion.

Whenever the parent says "we" when talking about his/her child's activity (as in "we are gunning for the state record for goals scored in the girls' soccer 10-and-under division"), it is another signal that a parent is overly involved. In other words, the parent identifies too directly with the child's accomplishments or failures. Obviously this tendency can be destructive, as it puts extra and often unwanted pressure on the young athlete. Little League Syndrome—that "disease" that occurs when parents, among other things, partake in backstabbing of coaches and in profane and even violent arguments at contests—usually stems from that basic misunderstanding by the parent as to whose activity it really is.

Parents must keep their emotional distance and let it be the child's own "thing" if that child is going to have a long and satisfying athletic career. An approach that puts the coach-athlete relationship front and center and allows motivation to be developed by and through the athlete—not imposed on him or her—will give that child the best chance to gain in all ways from the experience.

Support and Facilitate the Coach, but Let Him—or Her— Do the Coaching

Ideally, a parent will be aware of, and appreciate, the contributions a coach can make. Like a good teacher, an accomplished coach understands and works well with children, and can have a major positive impact on that child's evolution. If there is a choice, parents should check around for a coach and program from which the child will benefit. If there is only one option in that sport in your area, check the program out anyway. Satisfy yourself that there is far more upside than otherwise before signing up your child. Once you make the decision to go with the program, stay in the role of parent (a uniquely valuable role we will discuss in the next segment), trust the coaches, and let them do their best job of helping your child grow.

The Importance of Allowing Children to "Own" Their Sport

One of the most valuable aspects of a child's joining a youth sports team is that it is not a highly regimented "have to," like school. The child doesn't have to be in that program, so in that sense it is voluntary. Because it is voluntary, it is an incredible opportunity for the child to develop self-motivation. The quickest way for that to happen is for parents to allow their child to "own" the sport by keeping their hands off other than in a support-ing role. Don't communicate with them at all during practices except in an emergency, thereby allowing them to learn to handle, and eventually thrive in, a new social environ-ment. Allow them to develop an appreciation for their sport without you leading them through it. Allow them to develop a strong, positive relationship with another adult (the coach) on their own. Parents ultimately want their child to grow into an independent, self-supporting, self-initiating adult, correct? This is often the first real opportunity youngsters have to spread their wings and to discover that they have the power to improve and succeed on their own! Parents do their children no favors by closet-coach-ing them or overly regulating their child's sports experience.

A Coach's Role—A Parent's Role

How can both coach and parent ensure that a mutually beneficial and trusting relationship grows and flourishes? We have already defined the first step: Both parties must demonstrate reciprocal feelings of respect. We have also observed that the lion's share of this attitude stems from both parties recognizing that their shared objective, and that of the program, centers on the multidimensional development of the child's potential. This affirmative attitude concerning each party's significance in the develop-ment of the young athlete leads to the second major requirement for a suc-cessful relationship: mutual understanding, respect, and acceptance of each other's role. For parents, it's important to acknowledge that the coach is the technical expert and in charge of training and teaching the athlete. This is the "line" that defines where and when a coach is solely in charge. Parents *must* accept that premise if there is to be the greatest chance of unimpeded progress for their child. For coaches, they must recognize that this isn't their son or daughter, to do with solely as they see fit. Instead, the coach is an ally in developing the child, but the parent will always be pri-marily responsible for the child's evolution. To boil it all down: It's the coach's job to teach and train the athlete, yet the coach should treat her athletes as invaluable human beings as she does her part in helping guide them toward greater and continuing life growth and success.

It would seem obvious that both parties should accept their own role and respect the others'. However, this is not always the case. Some coaches distrust any parent having too much to do with the team, and extreme cases include coaches locking parents out of all practices and barring them from having anything to do with the team. Many of these coaches are merely misguided, but many have come by their rather extreme policies after having been burned by parents who do not respect boundaries. These parents shamelessly attempt to coach their child during practices or games, often (knowingly or otherwise) countermanding instructions the coach might have given. These conflicting messages can be horribly confusing for the child. On the one hand, the athlete is conditioned to follow the coach's instructions, yet who can go against one's own parents! What a vicious psychological Catch-22 for the child. In any case, the blurring of authority can only cause confusion and consequently poorer performances and experiences. A thorough understanding of both parties' functions is needed for these negative situations to be minimized. Let us now explore more thoroughly the role of coach and parent.

The Role of the Coach

As previously mentioned, the coach is in charge of all "on court" or "on field" responsibilities. That includes the planning and operating of all practices, creating and entering lineups, and making all decisions during contests. In general, coaches are the leaders, and it's their responsibility to plan and facilitate the development of each athlete during his or her time with the team.

Almost all parents will have at least a few questions as the season unfolds, and though some of these questions are easy to answer (like what to feed the child before a contest or when the new uniforms will arrive), others may involve issues that require a more detailed explanation. And even if a question seems ridiculous, listen! Show parents you respect them and appreciate their love for their child by hearing them out. In any case, communication between coach and parent is the key to surmounting or preventing any misunderstandings from occurring.

Because the parent cannot know all of the coach's broader full-season plans, misconceptions can arise. This is where a parent's trust in the coach comes into play, and why it is so critical. For example, nine-year-old beginning swimmer Betsy has learned the freestyle, yet does not know how to do a flip turn (the fastest type of freestyle turn). It would not be farfetched for a parent familiar with the sport to wonder why Betsy hasn't learned the flip turn yet. However, the coach has good reasons. Since Betsy will not be swimming a multi-length race for another two months and because the whole group does not know how to swim the breaststroke yet, the coach feels it is a better use of practice time now to focus on learning the breaststroke. The coach's timetable calls for flip-turn work to begin in two weeks. As this example illustrates, only the coach knows the needs of the whole group at any one time, based on his or her full-season master plan.

Here are a few ways to develop lines of communication with parents right off the bat:

- **Parent Meeting.** At the beginning of the season, have an informational meeting for all parents. First, explain your philosophy of coaching. Stress your commitment to developing positive habits and attitudes and that you emphasize *improvement* and *team* above all else. Then explain, in a non-threatening way, exactly what you would like from them, including any boundaries to be respected. An example of delineating boundaries might go something like this: "We welcome you to watch our practices. We know how special it is to be able to follow your child's progress like this. However, please do not interact with the coaches or your children during practice time, as both need to concentrate fully on the tasks at hand."

- **Communication Hours.** At the informational meeting define specific times when parents can reach and communicate with you or your assistants away from practices or contests. Then be sure you are available when you said you would be, and be patient and thorough in handling parents' concerns.

A Parent's Role

It is so important for young athletes that their parents stay just that—parents! Coaches and teachers come and go, but there are just two parents, and their position is unique. Parents are chief providers of food, clothing, and shelter, and usually the major emotional support in their child's life. In addition, parents know better than anyone their child's strengths and weaknesses, likes and dislikes, and special or unusual qualities. And last, but certainly not least, parents love their children unconditionally. However, if a parent is not the coach and starts to act like one, roles become blurred and signals crossed. The best way for a parent to function is to allow that child

---

Building Parents' Trust in Their Child's Coach

Coaches have many ways to display their professionalism and desire to help children grow, and numerous opportunities to do so. The following guidelines support the relationship between coach and parent by building trust and confidence that the coach has the best interests of the child at heart.

1. Openness: Allow parents to see (at practices and meets) how fairly, positively, and attentively ("My child really *is* important to this coach!") you treat their most precious possession.

2. Communication/Accessibility: By having parent meetings, initiating group informational e-mails, responding to questions through phone calls and e-mails, and maintaining office hours or other arrangements for parents to have time with you, you are opening and maintaining critical trust-building lines of communication.

3. Improvement: Your work ethic and total focus on helping the whole group improve will either be observed by your parents or heard about through their children. All are testaments assuring them that they have their son or daughter in a good program. Confidence and trust in the coach will continue to grow.

4. Professionalism: You conduct yourself in all ways as a good role model. You continue to educate yourself and show a deep understanding of the sport. As a professional educator who understands that your role is to help develop the child not just in sport but in life, you build your charges up, treat them in a positive, growth-oriented way, and treat them with unwavering respect.

---

to be guided by the coach and to stay in the background to share in their children's successes and be of comfort during the tough times.

In some organizations parents serve as coaches. This phenomenon occurs mostly in the "learn to" organizations, such as Little League baseball or local pee-wee soccer teams. Moms and Dads are asked to step up because the activity is at a beginning level and doesn't require as much expertise and/or the league could not survive without parent coaching. There simply aren't enough "professionals" to go around. However, even when parents do not coach, the team needs their help to function effectively. Parents are essential to the "off court" or "off field" aspects of running a team, such as setting up and operating phone trees, managing concessions, running contests and events, and overseeing other organizational functions. When parents handle these aspects, the coach can better focus on his or her main task. Parents will usually be more than eager to pitch in because their child benefits so much from the program.

The Game-Day Line-Up: A Valuable Teaching and Motivational Tool

The creation of game-day line-ups is a coach's responsibility. It's also a tremendous teaching and motivational tool.

The primary goal when creating a line-up is to give the team the best chance of winning. However, coaches often have an opportunity to create a win-win situation for their athletes. With thought and imagination, coaches can often change around athletes' events or positions within the lineup to create new opportunities for success, expose athletes to new situations, and to motivate them in new and different ways. One example is that of a high school swimmer who is a pretty good breaststroker, but only fifth best on her team, which means, since varsity meets often only have three entrants in any event, that she generally doesn't get a chance to compete at the varsity level. However, her coach sees that the opposing team has strong butterflyers and weak breaststrokers. This allows the coach to take two of his top breaststrokers (who are also excellent all-around swimmers) and move them to the butterfly event, while elevating the fourth and fifth breaststrokers to the starting line-up. New swimmers, therefore, get an opportunity while the team still makes out. Win-win.

Coaches in all sports have a plan of improvement for their athletes, and in many sports use entries and line-ups to create opportunities for improvement and success as the season progresses. This invaluable expertise comes from years of training and experience, yet, amazingly, there are many sports teams across the country whose coaches allow parents to decide what their son or daughter will compete in! I know of many swim clubs that allow such a practice. In such a case, the expert has allowed the amateur to make key decisions, *like a teacher who allows the students to decide what they will be tested on.* Don't be that coach who gives up such a learning/motivational tool.

The Destructive Parent

Before we get into the various ways parents can be supportive of their child and the team, let us first gain some perspective by exploring what it is like to be a *destructive* parent. The following factual account is reprinted from a 1984 *Los Angeles Times* article:

> "He was the fastest ten-year-old freestyler in the nation and he kept getting better. At twelve, he set a national record for his age. He was almost six feet tall, powerfully built, and had great flexibility and a natural feel for the water. His parents assumed he would be an Olympic champion.
>
> "But he stopped growing at thirteen and his improvement slowed. He hit a plateau at fourteen and could not drop his times. At fifteen he began to swim slower.

"His parents were furious. For nine years they had devoted their lives to swimming and they expected their son to win. They berated him constantly after meets and occasionally struck him after a poor swim.

He grew to hate swimming, but was afraid to tell his parents he wanted to quit. After years of spending up to five hours a day in the water pushing himself to exhaustion, years of frustration, years of listening to his parents tell him he was a failure, he attempted suicide by slashing his wrists.

'Both parents were . . . able to prove something, get some self-worth through their son's swimming,' said a Southern California swim coach who coached the boy for several years. 'When he swam slowly, they felt like failures. Whenever I want to put swimming in perspective, I think of that boy.'

This tale is a classic encapsulation of one of the major roads to "burnout" and a superb example of how the road to athletic excellence can sometimes be more damaging than helpful to a young life.

Some signs of a destructive parent include:

1. Living their life through their child.

Former athletes whose own careers fell short of their own expectations or parents who see potential stardom in their child are some of the types ripe for interfering in their young ones' athletic experience. This type of parent identifies more directly with their child's fortunes (*"We* won!" *"We* were cheated out of that game.") and thus often becomes overly caught up in the child's performance. This puts an additional and potentially counter-productive pressure on the young athlete. There generally is no long-term upside here—only a likely eventual rebellion by the child.

2. Having their own agenda (knowing what is best, despite the child's opposition).

Perhaps the father is a lawyer and feels his daughter should follow in his footsteps. Or the parents are champion bowlers; therefore, their son ought to be one as well. But wait. What if the son or daughter does not see it that way? Whose life is it anyway? On the one hand, signing a youngster up for an activity because the parents think it will be good for her—that's one thing. Signing children up for a variety of activities for fun, improvement, a sense of belonging, or just for some good, solid physical activity represents the kinds of decisions all parents make for the good of their children. That's parenting.

However, when a parent ignores what a child needs or wants and keeps that child in some activity for what is really the parent's sake—that's another thing. Ultimately, this kind of situation only hurts both parent and child. A variation on this theme involves parents who keep their child in a sport primarily as a means to get into, or pay for, college. In any case, if the child has been involved in that sport for many months or years and is being forced to participate, or to participate at a level where it isn't fun or satisfying any more, then the activity becomes a kind of slavery and is usually more destructive than constructive.

Symptoms of destructive parenting may include the following:

- **Placing blame.** A propensity by the parents to blame the coach for an athlete's poor performance.

- **Team hopping.** The changing of teams often, due to power struggles with the coach, conflicts with other team parents or teammates, sub-par performances by their child, etc.

- **A win-at-all costs attitude.** In this case their child's performance becomes magnified in importance, and hence, distorted. As a result, on game day, winning becomes paramount, improvement is no longer a focus.

I have seen numerous instances where young athletes perform brilliantly, but don't finish first. They'll approach their coach or parent with head hanging down or tears in their eyes because the *only* (parental) focus was to win! What a complete and utter distortion of what should be the main focus for any young athlete in competition—doing one's best! When a child cannot enjoy or even *recognize* that he performed his best that day, there is something seriously wrong.

Fortunately, these examples of destructive parents and their tendencies are the exceptions to the rule. Ironically, they usually spring from parental love and a sincere, if misplaced, desire for what's best for the child. Unfortunately, if parents become blind to their child's wants and needs, decisions will be made for the wrong reasons and possibly against the child's will. If you see sharply reduced motivation in your athlete and you can't figure it out, talk with the parents. Make sure you talk with them in private, away from the athlete. If need be, remind them that ultimately, for athletes to improve and succeed to the best of their abilities, they must take ownership of their sport.

The Positive, Constructive, Supportive Parent

A parent's unconditional love for his or her child and overwhelming desire to do what is best is assumed. However, what *is* best? What are the right decisions? How does a parent guide and support their children to give them the best chance of reaching their potential? Here are some guidelines that will help you give your child the best chance possible for positive, long-term growth.

1. Encourage your children; follow their lead.

Listen to their desires. Let them show you the pathways they are most eager to pursue by the enthusiasm they demonstrate. Be supportive, and let them experience the inevitable ups, downs, and plateaus inherent in athletics. Your child will show you he or she has passed the "internal motivation litmus test" when he or she reminds *you* to be ready to drive the carpool!

2. Teach your child always to try.

"Failure" is only temporary. We learn, advance, and broaden our understanding of all things by finding out what doesn't work as well as what does.

3. Allow your child to dream big dreams.

Don't burst the bubble. Visions of great things, no matter how improbable-seeming, often lead to more diligently following a coach's instructions, more disciplined practice habits, and more focused and specific goal setting. In short, from dreams evolves the desire to follow ones' dreams (which is *desire motivation*—the highest form).

4. Encourage your child to engage in other sports or kinds of physical activity.

Athletic ability is not merely genetic. It also comes from a child's developing a complete repertoire of sports skills (breadth of coordination, all-around strength and speed, balance, movement capabilities in all areas, as well as sports-specific concepts and motions). Each of these contributes to overall athletic potential, which can then be more fully exploited as the child matures. A friend of mine, a former swimmer, swim coach, and current sports psychologist, once noted, "Spending long hours stroking up and down a pool at a young age severely limits the development of a full range of sports skills and is a poor use of valuable developmental time. It can also be a prescription for early burnout." The same goes for excessive focus on any one sport at a young age.

5. Encourage your child to engage in non-athletic activities.

Any interest or activity such as the arts, debate, forestry, and so on, builds sports-related habits and skills, such as discipline, focus, and organizational skills, and also gives the child other perspectives for defining him- or herself. Being well-rounded is a good thing, for sports and for life.

6. Always keep the Big Picture in mind.

By keeping that mental image of how you want your child to be five, ten, fifteen years from now, you will tend to make the right decisions for the right reasons. Sure, being on top and garnering trophies left and right is fun at any age, but what is the price paid for such mono-focus? Burnout can be a terribly debilitating experience, as it can have negative ramifications not only immediately, but also far into the future in some cases. So keep all your actions and decisions focused toward long-range development of your child in all ways physically, mentally, socially, and emotionally.

This big-picture philosophy will keep you from, for example, signing up talented ten-year-old Kim for the traveling (advanced level) soccer squad against her will, because she isn't *that* into soccer, all her friends are on the "house" (lower level) team, she enjoys and wants to participate in a number of other sports, and she enjoys and is good at playing the French horn. Kim may be quite good at soccer, but if the extra motivation to do well isn't there, it is wise to tone down the soccer while opening up time and opportunity for other activities. Meanwhile, Kim will begin to compare and contrast her many interests while gaining a broad range of skills. Then, when she is a bit older and more able to decide for herself what she really wants to do, she will be more able to do so. "No" to burnout. "Yes" to positive development. You want children to be successful and happy. They can have both.

Behaviors of Supportive Parents

As previously discussed, parents are essential to the developmental growth of their children and should be involved at some level in their child's activities. This doesn't mean that they replace the child's teachers, doctors, or coaches. Instead, they must learn to work with the experts they've allowed into their children's lives. Just as children train to succeed in athletic events, often their parents must train for their roles as supportive parents. Here are a few ways, parents can express healthy support for their growing children.

Observing Practices

Practices of elementary and middle school sports teams are usually open for parents to observe, while high school practices generally aren't. For parents of younger age groupers, the following are some do's and don'ts when sitting in the stands or standing on the sidelines observing your son or daughter practice. Follow these suggestions, and you will get the most out of your time without interfering in any way:

1. Observe your child's practices with a philosophical attitude.

Just take it all in, the mistakes and the triumphs together, with the idea that you are watching your child evolve. Recognize that the road to major and long-lasting improvement is sometimes uneven due to developmental and other factors. As an example, sometimes a child gets "stuck," unable to pick up a skill for months. Then, seemingly all at once, the child catches on (see Chapters 7 and 8, which discuss child developmental stages). While the apparent lack of progress can be frustrating for a parent to witness, it is quite common and nothing to worry about. Be aware of, and enjoy watching, their social and emotional growth as well—not just their evolution vis-a-vis that sport.

2. Always assume that your child is trying.

Children love to please the person in charge, and they have a strong desire, in general, to improve. In fact, the only times I have seen children *not* try is either when they dislike what they are doing (in other words, they are either "have to" or "fear" motivated) or are having some issues with the coach. Not trying should be a red flag to the parent that something is wrong that needs immediate attention.

3. Do not interact with your child at practice.

Certainly parents should be able to watch their children practice. However, it is a good thing to not interact with them (unless in an emergency), because:

- The child cannot afford to receive mixed messages or be distracted.
- The child is learning and refining his or her ability to take instruction from other authority figures.
- Beginning age group athletes gain confidence in their ability to do things *without* their parents. They need to "own" their practice time as part of "owning" their identity as athletes.
- The coach is less inhibited and less distracted.

Coach and athlete use practices to develop their own working relationship. Each needs to feel free to do so. Parents who aren't able to respect and follow these guidelines should stay away from practice for their child's good and the coach's good.

4. Avoid sport-specific coaching of your child at all times.

It can be tough not to, but fight the urge, for it is infinitely more confusing for your child to be inundated with (often conflicting) advice. Instead, *ask* your child what is coming up at the next practice or how the workout went, and always be supportive of the efforts and sacrifices your child is making. Also, there are millions of "life lessons" you can slip in without directly coaching your child on sports-specific issues.

Being Supportive at Contests

Unlike practices, sports contests involving children of all ages are generally open to those who are interested in watching. Here are some ways a parent can get the most out of the experience while being supportive of both child and team:

1. Parental acceptance, no matter the result.

Your support for, and acceptance of, your child's efforts regardless of the results will be one of the most influential factors in his or her developing a healthy attitude about sports. For instance, when your child hasn't had a best performance in awhile, or when contests go poorly, she might feel down and disappointed. Instead of a tirade, expression of dismay, or lecture on working harder, give her a hug and express your pride in her efforts. Leave it to the coach to dissect the game or event and offer the technical critique. Remember, your reaction to a particular setback can often determine how long and severe the setback will be. At the other end of the spectrum, do not exult too loud or long over your child's record-shattering effort. That could signal to your child that she can only earn your love and praise by being the best. In any event, unconditional love and support will free up the child to do his or her best, and will help to avoid developing a fear of failure based on the specter of disapproval and family disappointment should he or she not do as well as hoped.

2. *Help your child learn to enjoy competition.*

During the car ride home, remind your child that he or she can learn and grow from mistakes and from coming up short, as well as from success. Encourage your child to set goals and surmount obstacles; point out that the fun is in accepting the challenge and then going after it!

3. *Cheer for and comment positively on the efforts of your child's teammates.*

The more voices that are cheering for anyone, the better that person or team will generally do. And, when parents and athletes are cheering together, there is an added dimension to the united feeling the team has. Most important, don't forget that children *love* to be complimented by an adult. When someone other than their parents or peers takes the time to notice and comment on that athlete's effort, the feeling can be quite special and is often remembered. Support your child's teammates and let them know how much you appreciate their efforts!

4. *Try never to compare your child with others, and certainly never do it when he or she is able to overhear.*

It's natural for parents to want to compare, but verbally doing so (especially if it is unfavorable) can damage the credibility of your unconditional support role.

5. *Tend to your child's physical and emotional needs.*

Making sure your child is adequately fed and clothed properly (uniform, extra clothes for colder weather, etc.), frees them from uncertainties or worries beyond the usual game-specific thoughts and butterflies.

No matter what, always try to be patient and supportive.

Do this and you will be giving your child's experience a huge boost!

▶ **Summary Points** ▶ ▶ ▶

▶ A coach's Foundation Attitude toward parents should (a) recognize the fact that the parent is an invaluable member of the greater team and that the child is all-important to the parent, and (b) that a coach's duty is not only to help develop the child in a particular sport, but also help develop the child as a person.

▶ A parent's Foundation Attitude toward their child's experience should be to (a) support and facilitate a child's participation while letting it be the child's own activity, and (b) support and facilitate the coach while letting him or her do the coaching.

▶ The Coach's Role: He or she is the technical expert in charge of the teaching and training of the athlete (i.e., in charge of all "on-field" or "on-court" responsibilities).

▶ The Parent's Role: He or she is the parent, responsible for all that such a unique role implies. Help out with "off court" responsibilities and be the best parent one can be, but allow the coaches to do their job to their professional best.

▶ Characteristics of supporting parents: Allow child to take ownership of their sport, always be supportive without interfering, and always try to keep the big picture in mind.

▶ Behavior of supportive parents: *Ask* the child how the practice or contest went, avoid sports-specific coaching, and provide unconditional support.

7

Child Developmental Stages: Kindergarten and Elementary School Years

A six-year-old's body is far more flexible than that of a sixteen-year-old, but has only a small fraction of the strength. To an eight-year-old athlete, "fun" is play and games, whereas to a fifteen-year-old, "fun" is more about the satisfaction of accomplishment and about accepting a challenge. The self-esteem level of the average five-year-old is generally much higher than that of a young adolescent. These are just a few examples of the changing nature of your athletes' realities, capabilities, desires, and needs, depending on how far they have evolved developmentally.

Up to this point in the book the concepts we've discussed have applied to all age group athletes, unless specific age ranges have been indicated. Still, it's important to remember that, though the message is universal, the methods, tricks, and emphases used when coaching different ages should vary due to differences in the child's development— physically, cognitively, socially, and emotionally.

This and the following chapter are devoted to better understanding athletes at different stages in their evolution. My good friend and colleague Dr. Anne Berenberg assisted me in the formulation of these two chapters, and deserves much credit for not only helping bring together such a range of information relating to child developmental stages, but also how such information can assist our efforts as coaches. In this first of the two chapters, we tackle the characteristics inherent in children from kindergarten through elementary school (approximately ages five through eleven). While reading both chapters, please recognize that though the *order* of developmental stages is the same for all children, the *rate* at which children develop varies. As an example, note the incredible differences in height, weight, and shape among the average seventh grade population. Also, during childhood we often see that one child may develop faster physically, yet slower-than-average emotionally and vice versa. In fact, children's growth rates may be affected by any number of factors, including illness or serious emotional stresses, such as family strife. There may be periods when a child's growth slows, followed by a period of rapid growth when the situation eases and they are catching up for lost time. [1] (To acknowledge these variations in child development, I have overlapped the ages connected with each stage slightly; e.g, the stage for elementary school ends at ages ten or eleven, and the middle school stage begins at ages ten or eleven. An informed view of the stages and variations in child development will help a coach in numerous ways. Perhaps most critically, it helps the coach to better understand why children are or are not performing what is expected of them. To make these chapters practical and accessible, they are designed so that first a developmental characteristic is examined, followed by discussion and advice from a coach's perspective.

Kindergarten (ages 5–6)

Picture This: You are walking toward the local elementary school one sunny Saturday morning, when you hear, not far away, the high-pitched voices of youngsters at play. As you draw nearer, you note that the sounds are coming from a first grade girls' soccer practice just getting under way. You pause to take it in and immediately stifle a chuckle at the fact that the coach is having a devil of a time keeping the attention of all the girls. He demonstrates a drill, then urges them to give it a try. Some kick the ball as demonstrated, but others are extremely awkward. One girl misses the ball entirely, then begins to wail at how stupid soccer is, while her buddies tease her. You notice with admiration how the coach quickly makes a comforting comment, encourages the disappointed youngster to try again, then congratulates her after she makes solid contact. The formerly (two seconds ago) crestfallen athlete beams and then begs to try it again.

After a few drills, the coach organizes a scrimmage, and you can't help noticing that, despite his best efforts at teaching proper positioning, the girls all bunch up around the ball, each trying to get her licks in. They all seem to be having a blast. As you start to walk away, your attention is drawn to one girl, who, after smacking the ball and starting to run after it, suddenly stops and heads to the sidelines. The coach entreats her to get back into the game, but she retorts "I'm tired, and anyway it's time for my snack."

•••

Have you ever wondered at what age a child is ready—physically, socially, and emotionally—to participate in organized team sports? I began to ponder this issue during my first coaching stint. I was assisting a summer swim team that included children ages five to eighteen. The five- and six-year-olds were cute and fun, but could they understand the larger picture? They seemed to be in their own little worlds, unable to understand strategy, sacrifice, and the rest of what makes up the team dynamic.

After years of coaching all ages, and after doing research and consulting experts in the field of child development, I've concluded that five- and six-year-olds can benefit greatly from team sports *if* the focus of the program is on the development of specific physical skills and general physical development, and the emphasis is on fun and play, *not* on competition. So let's take a look at some of the physical, cognitive, social, and emotional characteristics which make up the average five-and six-year-old.

Physical Characteristics

Overview

Five- and six-year-olds, or kindergartners, are extremely active and already have good general control of their bodies (running, jumping, turning, pushing). However, they are still discovering all that their bodies can do, and their ability to do even basic *specific* physical skills, such as kicking and throwing is evolving.

Tip 1: To get the most out of a child in this age group, focus on introducing and teaching correct technique of specific skills. This focus on skills, such as stepping, kicking, and then following through when addressing a soccer ball for instance, helps develop body awareness, which aids the child in becoming more in tune with his or her developing physical capabilities.

Tip 2: Keep your expectations grounded in reality by distinguishing skills that can be introduced (but not expected to be mastered at that age) from those that can be mastered relatively quickly. Know the skills in your sport that generally fit each of these categories, and you will automatically tailor your expectations more accurately to what your group can accomplish. Also, keep the presentation and instruction of these skills fun, interesting, and lively, using demonstrations, games, and other innovative methods.

Fatigue

Kindergartners are prone to bursts of activity and need to rest often. While they tire quickly, they often don't recognize the need to take a break.

Tip: This is one of a number of physiological and developmental reasons that sports sessions for the very young should be shorter than those for older athletes regardless of how advanced in that sport the young athlete may be. Try to keep practices moving, varied, and relatively brief and build short breaks into your sessions. Halftime during a scrimmage, water breaks, and instructional periods for explaining and demonstrating all qualify as the kind of short rest periods young athletes need.

Sex-Based Differences

Although boys are generally a bit bigger and slightly ahead in gross motor skills that emphasize force and power (such as jumping, running, and throwing), girls are actually slightly ahead of boys in just about all other areas of development (including fine motor skills, balance, and foot movement). Remember, however, these are statistical generalities. There are always exceptions.

Tip: As a coach, take care to avoid boy-girl comparisons or competitions between the sexes. As an example, society puts a lot of pressure on males to be the bigger, faster, and stronger sex. But a six year-old boy often isn't, and direct comparisons make it pretty tough on a boy who comes up short versus the girls.

Readiness

To a great extent, children at this age are either ready developmentally to (with practice) succeed at a skill, or not. In other words, DNA plays the major role in determining *do-ability*. That's not to say that children who are not as far along developmentally won't improve some with practice. However, the improvement will be in much smaller increments, and *exces-*

sive practice at what their body and brain aren't yet ready for can often create more frustration than progress. In general, children of this age can master large motor activities reasonably well but cannot master activities requiring a high degree of visual-motor or visual-spatial coordination. [2]

Tip: Many fathers hunger for their sons to show coordination and talent in sports like baseball and football at a young age and are often seen out in the backyard, working with them on their passing or hitting skills. It's a fabulous way to spend some quality parent-child time. However, nature decrees how far along the child will be developmentally. There is no evidence that a child this age, exposed to formal lessons *or* major backyard time, will move ahead significantly in motor skills. Almost all children will eventually master the skills you as their coach are teaching as they move along their own developmental path while continuing to practice. Think of your job as a guide. By teaching correct fundamentals and technique *even while they are challenged developmentally*, you are setting them up for major breakthroughs forward as their mind-body connections improve.

Hand-Eye Coordination

Children in this age group find it difficult to focus their eyes on small objects. Their brains find it hard to control input and output in several senses at once—like watching a ball (visual input) and moving their hand (motor output).[3] Therefore, many still have relatively poor hand-eye coordination.

Tip: This explains why T-Ball is the preferred form of organized ball at this age. It also reveals so clearly why coaches and parents should have a great deal of patience as well as lowered expectations regarding sports where hand-eye coordination is at a premium. Pushing for and expecting the acquisition of a skill the body is flat-out incapable of doing breeds nothing but frustration and disappointment for the coach and, especially, within the athlete.

Flexibility

Ligaments are more flexible and bones are softer in the young athlete. No wonder so many gymnasts start (and peak) so early in their lives. However, though the body in many ways may be more ready to succeed at such a sport, a child's psyche and emotional development usually are *ill-prepared* for the often intense, arduous workouts some coaches put them through to take advantage of that flexibility. For the child's sake, shorter practices at this age are best.

Tip: Generally speaking, young children bend but don't break as easily as older athletes. Nevertheless, a serious injury is a serious injury, no matter what the age. Make sure your athletes know your safety rules and that those rules are enforced.

Cognitive Characteristics

Overview

The nervous system, including the brain, is made up of interconnected neurons (or nerve cells). At the place that two neurons link up there is a minute gap, called a *synapse.* Chemical molecules, called neurotransmitters, pass from one neuron to the next. When a child is born, there are innumerable potential ways in which the nerve cells could connect with each other. Which potential pathways *actually* get used is largely determined by the child's experiences. Some potential pathways are used often and are strengthened as a result. Others are never used. Those that aren't eventually are pruned away and become unavailable.[4] Moreover, Hebb's Law (Donald O. Hebb, Canadian neuropsychologist) states that "cells that fire together, wire together." This is how memories are made. [5]

Tip 1: Coaches should be aware that neural pathways are strengthened by being used. Even relatively weak pathways can become stronger through practice. Thus, the child who initially fails to do an action well can often learn to do it automatically and appropriately by practicing. This is one reason to encourage *all* children. It is also a reason to teach the skill right in the first place and to praise children for making successive approximations to the desired movement. [6]

Tip 2: Hebb's "fire together, wire together" law means that children will come to associate certain emotions with certain experiences if they are often paired. Children who experience positive feelings while doing a sport or activity will naturally bring a positive attitude to their next encounters with it. On the other hand, children who feel shamed or threatened will find negative feelings evoked when approaching a similar situation. If children have already built up negative associations, these can't be reasoned away. It will take repeated positive experiences to rewire the pathways. These are extraordinarily important reasons for making sports fun and keeping the experience positive is at this age.

Imitation ("monkey see, monkey do")

When a monkey performs a series of actions, like peeling a banana, neurons in its brain fire prior to each action in the sequence. These same neurons, called "mirror neurons," also fire when the monkey watches another monkey peel a banana. Exciting new research suggests that an even more complex mirror neuron system exists in humans as well. When we see or hear someone kick a ball, it appears that our motor neurons fire *as if we were performing that action.* Our brains are wired to learn by imitating others, often without any conscious effort to learn and without putting it into words. [7]

Tip: Successful coaches demonstrate what they want the children to do, not just explain it in words. For most children, imitation will be the most powerful way of learning.

Concept of Team

Children this age still see things almost exclusively from their point of view. However, recent research has shown that, as opposed to being "stuck" at this stage and then suddenly jumping to the next, as had been previously thought, children's perspectives evolve slowly toward the ability to consider other points of view.

Tip: If thinking is mainly egocentric, then the whole idea of working together for the greater good, the very essence of the concept of *team*, is, at most, hazy at this age, and for many does not exist. So is there upside to team sports for children this young? Actually the upside is huge, if done well. First, all youngsters gain a feeling of belonging when they are part of a group. Second, by making it fun for them, a coach can help hook children into the sport, when in a few short years they will be capable of understanding the needs and goals of their team, thereby gaining more fully from the team experience. Third, and a less recognized benefit of team sports for the very young, is that they often become exposed to older athletes, either when they are on a team with older athletes (as exists with most youth swim teams, for instance) or when they practice or compete close enough to older athletes so that they can see their performance. Young athletes will tend to mimic the actions of the older athletes (some of whom become heroes to these young athletes) without even understanding why. They see older athletes working and sacrificing together, and, as if by osmosis, begin to internalize the team concept. Finally, because the five- and six-year-olds' perspective *is* evolving, the idea and meaning of *team* will begin to take hold, slowly but surely.

Attention Span

Young children have relatively short attention spans. They relish activity for its own sake, rather than as a means to an end. In fact, this period in a child's life corresponds to the latter portion of what is known as the "play years"—the period spanning ages two through six—when play is the dominant activity and supports every aspect of development. [8]

Tip: When planning practice sessions, *the more activity the better*. Plan thoughtfully, moving from one activity (drill, game, etc.) directly into another. Plan transitions between activities as well, and since children this age also need short, frequent rest periods to recharge the batteries, plan such transitions to include some rest. For example, after a short warm-up and some review drills, call a halt and allow the athletes a short rest while you explain and demonstrate the new drill for the day. Limit the time spent lecturing or having children this young stand in line. When verbalizing directions, short, clear explanations work best. And recognize that the younger the athletes, the more visually oriented they are apt to be, so make sure they can see how to do things, not just hear it. A five minute break, then back to the action!

Language.

By kindergarten, children are quite skillful with language, girls generally more so than boys. Most of them like to talk, especially in front of their peers.

Tip: At times a child will go into a long, rambling response to a simple question. When this happens, first acknowledge his or her point, respecting that person's effort. Then regain the momentum by redirecting the group's attention back to the task at hand. In general, be patient when gaining or regaining the group's focus, using such techniques as varying the loudness or pitch of your voice. Other effective attention-getting techniques include having them catch you in an obvious mistake while you are speaking or demonstrating, or immediately launching into a quick guessing game, such as "I'm thinking of an animal. . . . " They *love* guessing games and, in general, love to participate and be heard.

Comprehension (Keep It Simple)

Despite the fact that children at this age have come a long way with their language skills, their vocabularies and abilities to understand complex concepts are still quite limited.

Tip: Use words and concepts they can understand. Be simple and clear. Shun complexity. Take things step by step. Do not, however, use "baby talk," condescend, or in other ways talk down to them. Yes, they are young, and things need to be made simple and clear, but young athletes can sense if you are treating them as "less than." To be sure the message has gotten across, ask them to repeat it, or ask them if they understand. Generally speaking, you will have to repeat yourself more frequently with this age group.

Imagination

Imagination and inventiveness are at their peak at this stage of development.

Tip: It is easy to see why play of all kinds is the dominant activity and evolutionary mode for this age. Frame *drills* and *calisthenics* as *games* and *challenges* and continue to find interesting, imaginative, and innovative ways to express what you are doing.

Social Characteristics

Overview

Five-and-six-year olds generally show an eagerness to tackle new tasks, join in activities with peers, and, in general, find out their capabilities. An adult's allowing children the freedom to engage in activities as well as patiently answering their questions leads to more exploration and initiative on the children's part. Excessive restriction and impatience ("What you are doing is pointless") can often lead to children feeling guilty about doing things on their own.

As their capabilities advance, children at around age six move into another, related stage of development. Being permitted to make and do things, being allowed to finish what they have begun, and being praised for those accomplishments lead to a sense of "can do," of industry. Limitation and criticism lead to feelings of inferiority.[9]

Children do not learn or perform well when they are under stress. Being a little bit "pumped up" can lead to a positive adrenaline rush, but too much pressure or anxiety leads children to "shut down." They truly are incapable of using the higher levels of their brains. [10]

Tip: Who cares if the actions and activity of the very young athlete isn't perfect! The point is that they are stepping out, trying new things, and doing the very best they can. Praise what is praiseworthy and always encourage. This is truly a tender age. A teacher or coach needs to be a nurturing type: No drill sergeants or orderliness freaks need apply. If you don't have the personality or patience for this age, please do not inflict yourself on them! This is a great age of discovery. Don't shatter their self-confidence or diminish their capacity by threatening, criticizing, and punishing excessively. Build them up and watch them take flight!

Misunderstandings

Quarrels tend to be frequent, but are generally of short duration and quickly forgotten. These arguments tend to be over seemingly simple (yet important to them) things, such as possession or who goes first.

Tip: Always be consistent when meting out justice. Take care of the root of the quarrel immediately, but in a diplomatic, fair way, then immediately refocus the children involved and the group on the activity at hand. Disagreements will occur less often when the children are fully engaged, so plan your sessions with that in mind.

Emotional Characteristics

Overview

Five- and six-year-old children are not secure enough to handle the threat of failure. They tend to shut down and move to another activity when they are made aware that they lost or in some other way did not measure up.

Tip: Do *not* focus on winning and losing. In addition to the inability to handle failure emotionally, children this age are not as aware of the relative importance of the result of a contest (the main team goal being to win). They do not understand why they should care. What they love is the participation. As their coach, put yourself in their shoes and deemphasize winning, within yourself and in your program. Instead, focus on the exercise, the improvement in skills, and the fun that fires up five-and six year-olds to come back for more.

Open, Sometimes Angry, Expressions of Emotion

Five- and six-year-olds can calm themselves down when faced with minor stressors, but they are still of an age where they often express their emotions openly and without restraint. Angry outbursts, including crying, can be frequent. They occur more often when children are tired or hungry.

Tip: Do not overreact, and *don't* solve these situations by being overly strict and authoritarian. That's the easy way out. Though you may achieve your objective –a meek, compliant group—you'll have done major harm to your very young athletes by bludgeoning them into submission. You will have knocked out their curiosity and desire and replaced it with fear, guilt, and a feeling of inferiority. Not the best recipe for long-term growth and success!

Instead, if the situation does not improve immediately when you address it, give out-of-control youngsters a brief "time-out." Their removal will cause the group to operate more smoothly while irritated athletes get a much-needed breather. Often it's just a bit of rest that's needed, and, not wanting to be left out of the fun and action, they soon will pull themselves together, try to conform to behavior that is acceptable, and get right back into it. Since hunger is the other chief culprit of these breakdowns, emphasize to their parents that children should come to practices or games shortly after being fed and perhaps schedule a snack-and-water break midway through the contest or practice.

Fears

As mentioned before, children this young have incredibly vivid imaginations. Couple that with their constantly being exposed to new and strange situations, and it is easy to see why they may have fears of various sorts, including some highly irrational (to adults) ones.

Tip: In rare cases, children up to the ages of eight to ten can have these seemingly irrational fears. For example, years ago one of my nine-year-olds, after seeing the movie *Jaws,* did not want to swim the back-stroke for fear a shark might be lurking in the pool's deep end, out of sight, ready to make a meal out of her! It certainly is not uncommon for a five- or six year-old to want to avoid the deep end of a pool (even if they *can* swim), perhaps due to a simple fear of the unknown, of what cannot be seen or touched. Don't tease that child or force them into doing something they are terrified of (like forcing one's head under water when they cannot swim). Instead, let the child observe others doing that particular activity and allow him or her to come to grips with fears at his or her own pace.

Jealousy

Jealousy among young athletes for the affections of their coach tends to be common.

Tip: Simply do not play favorites. Instead, lavish attention on every athlete, thereby showing they are *all* favorites. This approach will almost completely wipe out extended periods of jealousy and will sharply reduce the number of shorter, temporary tiffs. It will also nip in the bud negative behaviors of children who act out intentionally to avoid being ignored.

Self-Esteem

Children in this age group are just beginning to form a sense of self-concept. Their self-esteem is generally high, as they are constantly learning and discovering new things, are growing and becoming more accomplished each day, and because they only have a hazy idea of how competent they are vis-à-vis others.[11]

Tip: This positive sense of self-ability is nurtured and supported by the patience and encouragement of the key adults in their lives. We don't want to squelch their sense of excitement and curiosity *or* their positive sense of self. Don't feel you should point out all of the mistakes they make just for the sake of honesty. (They are often unable to take much criticism, constructive or otherwise.) Instead, point out what they do well, encourage them, and gently redirect or correct them when necessary. The "compliment sandwich" (mentioned earlier in this book) is one very effective way of making sure the child takes your constructive criticism the right way. `

Elementary School (ages 6–7 to 10–11)

Picture This: "Hey, batter, batter . . . toss that pea in there . . . she can't hit the side of a barn!" The sounds of energetic, chattering youngsters fill the air at a typical Little League baseball game. Out in the field, the visiting team keeps up a constant barrage of advice and encouragement to the pitcher, while ribbing the opposition. At the plate is one of two girls playing for the home team, but the fact she is a girl doesn't protect her from the (mostly) good-natured insults that occasionally fly her team's way. In and around the home dugout, some players are cheering for their teammate, others are comparing baseball cards ("I'll trade you Jeter for Pujols straight up"), a couple are racing each other to the drinking fountain, and three not in the game have wandered behind the stands to check out a gopher hole. The batter tags the next pitch, and as it zooms toward right field, the first baseman makes a desperate but futile attempt to snare the ball. He kicks the ground angrily, then dejectedly shuffles back to his position, though even Albert Pujols himself couldn't have reached that line shot.

Such are some of the sights, sounds, and actions that signal the developmental level of athletes of this age.

Physical Characteristics

Overview

In general, the average North American child will weigh around forty-five pounds at age six and eighty pounds by their eleventh year. Here's another interesting fact: At six years of age the human brain has grown to ninety-five percent of its eventual size.

Tip: In swimming, when teaching the streamline entry or push-off position (arms extended, head down, hands on top of each other, top hand's thumb "locked" around the bottom arm's wrist; forming what looks like a spear) to younger athletes, we often have to alter the position of their arms relative to their head. We ask these athletes to place their arms on the back of their head instead of on either side. Why? Since their heads are so large relative to the rest of their bodies, their arms will bow out too much if placed on either side of the head, thus severely compromising the goal of a slim, streamlined body line. As they grow older and their arms lengthen, we shift the positioning of the arms. This is a super example of how, depending on an athlete's age, body type, or other factors, coaches must be flexible in what and how they teach.

Bone and Ligament Development

At this age, bone growth is still far from complete. Therefore, bones and ligaments cannot stand heavy pressure. Ligaments are also not yet firmly attached to bones, which helps explain why children have greater flexibility than adults.

Tip: In team sports, for instance, baseball, encourage rotation of especially tiring positions, such as pitcher or catcher. Obviously, greater flexibility is the major reason gymnastics coaches want to start athletes at younger ages. That is okay, so long as spotting (when a coach stands next to the athlete with hands out, physically helping the athlete through the move or providing support if necessary) is superior and the sport remains fun. Flexibility can be maintained through stretching and other exercises without piling on the workload excessively.

Motor Coordination

Early in this period large-muscle coordination is still superior to fine-motor coordination. For instance, a young swimmer will usually have a decent kick (large muscles), while it can be a challenge to coordinate the correct arm stroke with the correct timing of the breathing. By age ten, though, fine-motor coordination has become quite good. Also, many children still have difficulty focusing their eyes on smaller objects. Such difficulties may continue until about age eight. During this period, the brain becomes more and more able to coordinate input and output of several senses at once, paving the way for improvement in sports like tennis and baseball. [12]

Tip: Be patient with those who "fumble around" more than their peers. These children may be having problems with their eyes, or their coordination might be lagging, but, in most cases, their relative ineptitude in your sport primarily will be due to developmental reasons, provided there is no lack of effort.

Tip: Repeated practice helps skills become automatic, strengthening neural pathways. But it's important to remember that the brain responds to novelty, so plan lots of variety in your practices. Also, as learning specialist Jane Healy notes, "Synapses [the points where neurons connect] get 'tired' with repeated use over a long period of time. They need a short rest to become effective again. Changing activities for awhile unblocks the pathways." [13]

Energy

At this age children are extremely energetic and active. Continuing lung growth allows more air (fuel) into the system, which enables children to exercise longer and more vigorously without tiring as fast.

Tip: Sports are a great way to release that seemingly inexhaustible energy. As with the five- and six-year-olds, do not keep them still or in a line for long periods of time. As a general rule, the amount of time they will be able to be still while watching and learning, or while receiving instruction, will increase with age. As with the five- and six-year-olds, do not hold them in a line or otherwise keep them still for long periods of time. Plan well and keep practices moving.

Absences Due to Illness

The common illnesses of childhood–colds, measles, strep throats, viruses—occur most commonly through age nine..

Tip: For this reason frequent absences from your practices may occur for some athletes. Be prepared for this fact and be flexible and innovative with any attendance expectations and requirements. Also, remind your athletes of cleanliness procedures, basic nutrition, and the value of getting enough sleep; and make sure all your athletes know to stay home if they catch a communicable disease.

Safety

Children in this group tend to be extreme in their physical activities. They have great control of their bodies and develop considerable confidence in their skills. Therefore, they sometimes are a bit reckless and underestimate the dangers involved. Statistically, the accident rate is at its peak in the third grade. By age nine or ten, boys forge ahead of girls in strength and endurance and enjoy rough play so much that they often injure themselves.

Tip: Safety is an issue for all age groupers, but especially this age. Define safety rules from the start, let both children and their parents know that safety rules are nonnegotiable, and repeat these instructions several times during the season. Have a first aid kit available, know how to use it; and, if you are in charge, make sure your assistants are well-versed in its use as well. Finally, enforce simple safety rules, such as no running on deck (swimming) during practices and games.

Puberty

Some girls start to reach puberty before age ten, though the average is around twelve years of age. Boys start puberty on average a couple years later.

Tip: This is another variable that helps us understand how and why our athletes differ in terms of size, strength, coordination, and mental and physical maturity. Regarding those girls or boys who reach puberty early, *never ever* single them out and call attention to their changing physiques. They are hyper-aware and self-conscious about themselves as it is.

Nutrition

Children this age do not pay much attention to good nutrition and tend to eat sporadically. Roughly a third of elementary school youngsters suffer from obesity, and that percentage has been rising in the United States.

Tip: Give them basic nutritional information and encourage them to put "high octane fuel" into their systems. When appropriate (say, during contests) give the children nutritional snacks or ask the parents to do so. Except on rare occasions, refrain from rewarding children with junk food, or your good nutrition message will become twisted.

With regard to the overweight children in your program: Since they tend to have self-image issues, anything positive you say can have an especially beneficial effect on them.

Cognitive Characteristics

Overview

As children mature from seven to eleven, they become able to process information ever more quickly and effectively. Because they're more efficient thinkers, they can take in larger amounts of information. They also begin to use memory strategies to retain new information and transfer it to long-term memory. First they learn to use rehearsal (repeating new information over and over), then organization (grouping together related pieces of information), and finally elaboration, or synthesis (creating a relationship between two or more pieces of information that hadn't been connected before).[14] As they develop these memory strategies, they become able to learn, remember and apply strategies for playing their sport.[15] From early mid-childhood on, the child becomes far more able to understand directions and take instruction. Recent research has shown that the forms of logic required to understand and follow through on directions do not emerge exclusively as a result of predetermined brain maturation, but are also socially generated as an outcome of practical activities.[16]

Tip: The more practice a child has in using logical thinking skills, the more those neural pathways are strengthened. Therefore, sports situations in which children are adding, comparing, evaluating, following instructions, and performing other mental exercises help a child become more cognitively able.

Concept of Team

Children are increasingly able to consider the viewpoints of others. They are becoming more aware that others may have different wants, needs, feelings, and experiences than they do—their theory of mind is becoming more sophisticated. They are starting to be able to view their own behavior from the perspective of others.[17]

Tip: The ability to understand where their fellow athletes are coming from is critical to the development of a sense of team, as well as the ability to get along with each other in such a structured environment.

Attention/Focus

As typically developing children move through the elementary school years, their capacity for attention and focus increases. They become less impulsive and more able to plan. They are developing what is called *executive functioning:*

> (a) Attention becomes more *selective.* Children are more able to pay attention only to those aspects of a situation that they decide are important, ignoring those irrelevant to the task at hand. (For example, a child will look at the coach's demonstration and not become distracted by his untied shoelace.) This aspect of attention improves greatly between the ages of six and nine years. (b) Focus becomes more *adaptable.* Children now tend to flexibly adjust their attention to the momentary requirements of the situation (e.g., "I know *this* but I do not know *that,* so I will focus on learning *that* to improve."). (c) A child's ability to *plan* increases. Children now can weigh alternatives, decide what to do first, next, and so on, and organize their thoughts into strategies.[18]

We will discuss executive functioning further in the section on adolescence.

Tip 1: The bottom line here is that five- and six-year-olds tend to *react;* but as they age, they start to *plan.* Kindergarten-age children generally do not have the ability to pay attention with enough cognitive functionality to understand the intricacies of a sport and cannot pay attention for long enough anyway. By age seven or so, they generally can. This is huge for learning and progressing, especially in team sports such as basketball, hockey, and soccer.

Tip 2: Some children lag far behind their peers in their ability to focus and sustain their attention, to control their impulses, and to manage their activity level. Often these children will be diagnosed as having Attention-Deficit/Hyperactivity Disorder (ADHD). For this type of athlete you'll need to keep instructions short, directions simple, rules clear, and activity level high to keep them constructively engaged. Sometimes they need extra attention from an assistant coach. Remember that they generally aren't trying to be disruptive, and their energy can be an asset to the team. [19]

Standards and Realistic Objectives

Elementary school children aren't skilled at setting goals for themselves, then monitoring their progress toward those goals. It's hard for them to judge what is realistic to expect from themselves. It's also hard for them to monitor their progress toward goals, checking how well they've performed the intermediate steps, then redirecting their efforts if they aren't having the desired results. This executive function is called *cognitive regulation,*[20] and will be much more operative in adolescence. Some children set unrealistically high standards for themselves, and frequently the inability to live up to such standards leads to frustration and guilt. Other children may seem to have fairly attainable goals but are clueless about how to go about achieving them.

Tip: Coaching, in the truest sense, will help children of this age. A coach should help focus the child toward the goal at hand; help keep them on track. Because they are not yet fully functional at cognitive self-regulation, they will tend to have difficulty with goal setting and monitoring. Nevertheless, during the later elementary school years, you can begin the process of teaching them how to set realistic short, intermediate, and long-term goals, and monitor and remind them as they gradually acquire the ability to goal-set and monitor themselves.

Also by breaking down major objectives into a series of shorter, more reachable goals, all your athletes will begin to view the same progress as "continued success" instead of "not close yet." For example, a very good nine-year-old swimmer set her sights on the state championships. The qualifying time for her event was 42.0 seconds, but her best time, with about four months left to qualify, was a 45.7, meaning she'd have to drop nearly 4 seconds from her personal best to get the chance to compete. After the first month of practice, she swam a 44.4. If she'd had no shorter-term goals, she might have felt that she was still way off her ultimate goal and might have been inclined to feel dejected and defeated as a result. Instead, her coaches helped her set one-month goals of 44.7, 43.7, and 42.8 on the way toward that 42.0 qualifying time. Therefore, that 44.4 she just swam actually exceeds her first month goal of 44.7, and causes her to feel successful and on track.

Language

Children like to talk, especially the younger ones in this age grouping (see page 138 on cognitive characteristics of five- and six-year-olds). They still have more facility with speech than with writing and are eager to recite and give answers.

Tip: Every so often have them feed back the answer to you. Occasionally have them respond to certain technique or game situation-type questions. It is a great technique for keeping them on their toes and helping them feel good about their knowledge.

Nonverbal Communication

Children continue to develop their nonverbal communication skills throughout elementary school. They will notice more cues—facial, gesture, and context—that help them become more adept at interpreting the full range of what others are communicating, including emotional state, and feeling. They also begin to notice when words and body language or facial expression don't match and can begin to tell jokes.

Tip: Ever wonder why teachers and coaches of kindergartners are so expressive verbally and physically and why teachers and coaches of middle school athletes generally aren't so voluble? (Of course moms won't wonder—they instinctively are more expressive to their children the younger they are.). Once children improve their nonverbal skills, they no longer need dramatic forms of communication to understand the message. They are also able to at least begin to get your jokes (finally), for the same reason!

Social Characteristics

Overview

It is during the elementary school years that children relish tackling tasks and feel a great sense of accomplishment when they do. They are curious about most everything and eager to learn. However, if they fail or are called a failure, they tend to feel inferior and are quick to sulk or withdraw.

Tip: As previously noted, one of a coach's most important objectives should be to help their athletes move up the motivation chain so that as many as possible become motivated primarily from within. Since a child at this age tends to be eager and energetic already (though generally in short bursts), coaches should jump on this opportunity! Take that natural "I want to try" attitude and build on it. Give them do-able drills and tasks and watch them eat them up! Use the *mastery* approach (i.e., try not to compare them with others, but instead work with them at their own level and have them focus on their own improvement). Be truthful, but accentuate the positive to help them realize they are succeeding. By emphasizing that their own mastery is what is most important, children will focus less on how they compare with their peers, and feel better about their own accomplishments.

Peer Group

As children advance in age through this period, the peer group becomes more a fact of life as well as an increasingly powerful influence. The peer group becomes a very important context for learning about how to get along with others—how to give and take, how to follow spoken and unspoken rules, how to adapt to the wishes of others, how to assert oneself, and how to understand what others are thinking—as well as how to evaluate oneself.

Tip: There are few better ways to positively satisfy a youngster's needs for peer interaction, approval, and acceptance, than by being a part of a team. The team serves as a haven, a place where the child bonds and feels he and she belongs. *But what should you do if the child feels left out, or if the team or group shuns a child? Coaches have quite a few options for integrating these children:*

- Put extra effort into subgrouping them with others they are similar to, or with those who are generally more tolerant.
- Find out if the child has any friends on your team, and put them in the same group or on the same side if it is positive to do so.
- Help them find new friends.
- And always, as the leader, be inclusive. Use your status and author-ity to encourage all your team members to embrace, or at least accept, each other as worthy human beings of value to the team.

Believe me, it works. Most of the swim teams I have coached included ath-letes aged five-or six up through the mid- to late teens. Some of the many ways we used to create more team unity included encouraging our older swimmers to take interest in the younger ones and by often involving all ages and ability levels when having relay races or playing certain games Also, by having occasional team meetings that involve all skill and/or age levels, we could emphasize the importance of all our team members to the success of the team, not just in the scoring of points, but in so many other ways. Lavish attention on any and all athletes who are trying, regardless of age or ability.

Sense of Fairness

During the elementary school years, children have moved from a concept of fairness that is strictly equal in distribution ("you get to use that toy, now I get to use it") to one based more on merit. By age eight or so, their concept of fairness includes giving special consideration to those who are younger or otherwise disadvantaged.[21]

Tip: Practice sessions for most sports are generally built around the idea that if development is to occur, some organization and order must exist. During soccer or basketball drills, sometimes children must stand in line and wait their turn; when learning a new wrestling move, one of the paired wrestlers will learn it first, then the other. Looking back for a minute at the preschooler, most five- and six-year-olds are fine with this fair method of taking turns. However, if speedy soccer player Jake goes first because he is the fastest and the drill will go more smoothly if the faster players are not held up by slower players going before them, then arguments are sure to break out. However, children in elementary school will be more aware of *why* Jake should go first. And given a couple more years will even buy into why Desmond will go first once in awhile, even though he is quite slow or physically challenged.

Please be warned, however, that your athletes are still *developing* their sense of fairness and do not yet understand or accept why certain practice structures or methods exist. Therefore, discuss specific situations as they occur. Put out brushfires by being fair. Explaining to them why you handled things in such and such a fashion will help children better understand the concept of fairness, which in turn will cause them to feel less resentful. They will learn that there are very good reasons why the coach benched them or put them in a particular order. As a result, they will learn to trust you, the coach, and complain less. In any given season, I will have a few nine- and ten-year old swimmers who *still* get into tiffs about who should go before whom. They take it personally. Though part of their mind understands, their ego has a hard time dealing with it.

The key here is to patiently take the few extra seconds necessary to concisely explain the reasons for the decision. Do so by taking the child to the side, one-on-one whenever possible, so he or she won't feel embarrassed in front of the group. In addition to helping that child to better understand the immediate situation, your making that extra effort will pay major dividends down the road. To use business parlance, you will be *growing your relationship* by treating your athletes with such care and respect.

Hero Worship

Crushes and hero worship are common. Idols may be rock stars, sports figures, and sometimes the coach.

Tip: Strong hero worship can often result in the athlete almost blindly following the coach in thought and action. For this reason it's critical that we are aware of our influence and strive to be positive role models at all times. Also be aware that a hero-worshipping athlete is highly motivated, if for no other reason than that he or she wants to please. Harness that desire!

Competition

Especially among boys, competition, boasting, and quarrels may be common.

Tip: Express your competitive philosophy at every chance (see Chapter 4, Competition). Counsel your athletes to compete *with*, rather than *against*, one another and to measure improvement mainly vis-à-vis oneself. Praise them in front of their peers. And remind them to be gracious in both victory and defeat.

Emotional Characteristics

Overview

Children now are becoming more alert to the feelings of others, though not as aware of *how much* it hurts or feels good. As a result you often see youngsters hurt each other deeply by attacking a sensitive spot ("Hey slowpoke!"). At the same time, these children are quite sensitive to criticism and ridicule, and they may have difficulty adjusting to failure. Their greater cognitive capacity to evaluate themselves can lead to painful self-assessments.[22] Self-esteem drops as children compare their own abilities to those of their peers, and as they are exposed to and can better understand the opinions of others.

Tip: Idyllic childhood? Sometimes we tend to forget how tough this age was emotionally. When forced to think back on my early years, I do remember hurtful nicknames and spiteful comments that could sometimes shatter my day and erode my confidence. As a coach, you have the opportunity to make your team a haven for *building* confidence and self-esteem, not just by helping children improve in their sport, but also by promoting a team culture of "unity," in which team members build up and support each other. First, help them understand that tearing down one's teammate is counterproductive to a successful team, both in emotional and performance terms. Second, find truthful reasons to praise *each* of your athletes; do it often, and encourage your team members to do the same for each other. Third, avoid labeling, ridicule, and sarcasm scrupulously, and don't allow that behavior in your athletes.

Emotional Regulation (Managing Strong Feelings)

Starting at age six, most children show notable gains in managing their feelings as they mature. They gradually develop techniques for calming themselves down when they are upset. Six- or seven –year-olds may still cry, however, when their feelings are hurt or exhibit rage when they are angry. Showing increased emotional regulation, ten-year-olds may be able to problem solve or to turn to a friend for support when they feel that they have some control over the outcome of the situation. ("Let's go together to the first practice so we don't feel scared.") At those times, when they feel the outcome of the situation is beyond their control, ten-year-olds may even be able to use techniques like breathing deeply, distracting themselves, walking away, or talking positively to themselves to reframe the situation ("I didn't win the race, but I made an awesome flip turn."). [23] Younger or less mature children will need more cues from the coach about ways to handle emotional upsets than will more mature children.

Tip: Because athletes this age are *developing* emotional management skills, they will still need guidance and support at times to figure out an appropriate response, as well as positive reinforcement when they do handle situations in an emotionally mature manner.

Self-Esteem

The judgments we make about our own worth and the feelings associated with those judgments are what make up self-esteem. Beginning in the elementary school years, an increasingly strong relationship exists between self-esteem and everyday behavior.[24] Significantly, experiences that reinforce a negative view of self will contribute to a downward spiral in self-esteem, while positive experiences will help create an ever-improving sense of self-worth.

Tip: Organized sports can have a really beneficial effect, not just on an athlete's sport-specific performance but also on his or her overall sense of pride and worth as a person. Because many psychologists separate self-esteem into the three subcategories (academic, social, and physical) to better understand *the root* of a child's esteem issues, it should be recognized (and shouted from the rooftops) that gains in one area often have substantial beneficial effects on another—i.e., the crossover effect. For example, many times I've heard parents go on and on about how their son or daughter, after succeeding that summer in our program, showed substantial improvement in school the following fall. Imagine the good your program can do for athletes of this age! Just as these children are leaving the "self-centered" focus of early childhood to enter the big, bad world of understanding others' sometimes negative view of them, they join *your* program, a haven for esteem building! So how does one create such an environment?

Creating a Positive, Supportive Athletic Environment

The coach, like any teacher, has an incredible opportunity to shape children's lives. Children who learn to tread water, shoot a basket, or kick a soccer goal are usually so proud of their accomplishments that they demonstrate it repeatedly to their coaches, parents, and friends. Their mastery of one simple skill boosts their self-confidence and esteem so high that it crosses over to other areas of their lives, tamping down fears and anxieties about learning their multiplication tables or writing a paragraph, for example. Creating a positive, supportive environment for learning involves a couple of crucial elements.

Emphasis on Self-Improvement

By focusing athletes on their own individual improvement rather than their placement vis-à-vis others, a coach can help the child feel more in control of his or her destiny. Teach your athletes ways they can ascertain and monitor their improvement. In some sports (track and field, speed skating) measuring athletic progress is relatively easy (time, distance, height, and so on). With regard to the more subjective sports such as figure skating, and team sports in general, monitoring one's own progress is not quite as clear-cut. Yet the athlete can still measure certain aspects inherent to that sport or position. For example, though much of what a defensive lineman does in a football game is not measurable per se, he still needs speed and strength (40-yard time, bench press weight), and part of his game performance *can* be tallied, such as the number of tackles, sacks, or fumble recoveries. But what about those areas of an athlete's game that can't be so readily measured? That's where a coach's observations of the athletes and communications of what was observed are so important to helping them understand the progress they are making.

Short-Term Goals

Yes, we know that children at this age struggle when it comes to figuring out what are realistic goals and in monitoring their progress. But some do fine, and all will benefit if you are there to advise them on what is challenging, yet realistic, and to remind them of their objectives. Emphasize short-term goals since it is so difficult for a child at this age to think and evaluate what he or she might be capable of months down the line. The effect of setting and then realizing a goal, any goal, will give an athlete a sense of accomplishment as well as an increased confidence that he or she can achieve the next goal, and the next.

The Crossover Effect: The Benefits of a Positive Environment

The focus on one's own improvement and the successful setting and achieving of short-term goals in sports aids the development of physical self-esteem. What about the other two self-esteem categories mentioned earlier? From a social perspective, as children begin to succeed they usually tend to feel more comfortable in and around their sports-specific peer group. They feel more worthy and accepted. Often their increased self-confidence and comfort starts showing up in other social and peer situations.

And the academic arena? How can succeeding in age group sports have a positive effect on academic self-esteem? Directly, perhaps not a lot. One does not tend to learn algebra on a baseball diamond. However, the habits of success an athlete learns in sports can be used in the academic world with great effect: desirable habits such as effective time management, goal setting, and so on. Let's also remember that success in one area will tend to bolster one's confidence in general. Through what they learn and the challenges they overcome in your sports program, young athletes are sure to feel far more capable of tackling *anything*!

> ▶ **Summary Points** ▶ ▶ ▶

▶ When working with children, coaches should develop programs using methods based on the athlete's age and developmental level.

▶ This chapter covers the first two of the four child developmental stages: kindergarten (ages five and six) and elementary school (ages six and seven through ten to eleven).

▶ All children develop in the same *order*. However, there are differences in the *rate* at which they develop Each stage is examined from four different aspects of development—physical, cognitive, social, and emotional.

▶ By becoming familiar with the stages of, and variations in, child development, a coach will better understand why children are or are not performing what's expected of them.

▶ Coaches can help young athletes increase their overall self-confidence and self-esteem by creating a positive environment that produces a crossover effect.

Notes

1. Harrison, Alexandra, M.D. Interview in March, 2006.
2. Healy, Jane, 52–53.
3. Healy, Jane, 52–53.
4. Solms, Mark & Turnbull, Oliver, 8–11.
5. LeDoux, Joseph, 214–216. Solms, Mark & Turnbull, Oliver, 145–146.
6. Healy, Jane, 37.
7. Iacobini, Marco, pp.3–46.
8. Berk, Laura, 294.
9. According to Erik Erikson's conceptualization of the "Eight Ages of Man," five and six year olds are moving from the stage of "Initiative vs. Guilt" to the stage of "Industry vs. Inferiority." See 255–261 for his description of those psychosocial stages.
10. Dykema, Ravi. For a highly technical discussion, see Porges. See Le Doux , 289, for the effects of emotional arousal on concentration. See Solms & Turnbull, 168, for a discussion of the impact of high stress or fear on memory.
11. Berk, Laura, 369.
12. Healy, Jane, 52–53.

13. Healy, Jane, 100.
14. Berk, Laura, 445.
15. The term "*metacognition*" is used to describe the capacity to "think about thinking," which develops during the school years. This capacity to sit back and consciously strategize enables children to become ever more sophisticated athletes.
16. Berger, 356.
17. Berk, Laura, 492–493.
18. Berk, Laura, 443–444.
19. See Barkley for a thorough discussion of how to work with children who have AD/HD.
20. Berk, Laura, 445.
21. Berk, Laura, 494–496.
22. Berger, KS., 358.
23. Berk, Laura, 491.
24. Berk, Laura, 486.

Child Developmental Stages: Middle School and High School Years

Middle School (ages 10–11 to 14–15)

Picture This: "Take your marks . . . Beep!" The last heat of the Girls' 11 to 12-Years-Old 100-Yard Freestyle Event has just begun. Prior to the start, it was noted that a few of the girls appeared almost full grown and as big, if not bigger, than the average boy of the same age. The next few heats involve eleven and twelve-year-old boys, yet the difference in size among the boys is even more startling. Most of the boys in the fastest heats are generally far bigger and more muscular than their peers, though there are several exceptions. There's a lot of down time between events at these meets, and girls and boys generally keep separate from each other, though one can see that some of each sex are furtively checking each other out from time to time. Mostly (between events) boys are seen running around with each other, exploring, goofing around, or just playing with computer games, while the girls sit in small groups, jabbering with each other, texting, or listening to music.

Puberty, the term given to our body's physical transition to adulthood, is the signature event of early adolescence, which generally coincides with the middle school years. Both boys and girls experience major physical changes over a short period of time. In general, girls reach puberty a couple years before boys, and it can begin as early as eight or nine years of age (and in rare cases even earlier). For both sexes, the age at which puberty begins varies. However, the sequence of physical changes is the same. The first outward sign of puberty is the growth spurt: a rapid gain in height and weight that generally starts in girls around age ten and for boys about age twelve. Interestingly, growth is uneven. Hands, legs, and feet accelerate first, and the torso follows, which is why many adolescents appear ungainly and feel awkward. Shortly thereafter, the development of sexual characteristics begins, such as breast and hip development and the beginning of menstruation in girls and penis development and the beginnings of facial hair growth and voice deepening in boys. These are changes of such magnitude and uniqueness that, although the term *puberty* refers only to the physical changes that take place, its impact on adolescents socially and emotionally is profound.

Physical Characteristics

Overview

Adolescent boys add roughly nine inches during their growth spurt, while for girls it's more like six to seven inches. The majority of growth may occur in a year or less but usually continues for two or three years. Because the starting time and length of growth spurts differ so much from person to person, variations in size and the rate of change can be tremendous. Girls are generally taller and heavier than boys through much of the middle school years, but by age fourteen the typical boy has surpassed the typical girl in height and weight.

Tip 1: In general, early adolescence is a great time for pursuing athletics. Most changes, such as increases in height and strength, tend to improve athletic capability. This is especially true of adolescent boys. Therefore, when evaluating a middle school athlete's performance, keep an eye out for how much of the athlete's improved performance is due to a growth spurt, instead of increased effort or improved technique. This must be factored in when assessing whether an athlete is tapping in to the greater part of his or her potential.

Tip 2: Conversely, an athlete may be one of the hardest workers on the team, yet measurable improvement may be small because that athlete isn't currently growing. Also, not all physical changes aid performance. This is especially true for girls, where weight and proportion changes can create extra challenges in many sports such as gymnastics, figure skating, and swimming. A coach's understanding of the frustration athletes feel in being temporarily stuck in a "plateau" state is key to communicating and motivating them. Make them aware that even very small increments of improvement are significant and meaningful to you. Also, emphasize their wonderful work ethic, leadership skills, or other great qualities both privately and in front of their teammates.

Self-Image

All this physical change usually means that adolescent athletes will begin to feel very self-conscious about their appearance. Couple that with the fact that young teens are constantly bombarded with glamorous and mostly unrealistic images on TV and in the popular media, and it's no wonder their self-image might take a hit.

Tip 1: The great thing about participating in athletics at this age is that children will tend to more readily and seamlessly adjust to, and become more comfortable with, their rapidly changing physiques. Why? First, often sports uniforms reveal more of one's body than everyday clothes. Yet because all athletes in that sport wear the same thing, it's viewed as normal and okay, and the focus stays on the sport, not the individual and what he or she looks like. Second, because athletes use their bodies so much, *action* becomes more important than *appearance*. The focus is more on how one performs, not on how one looks.

Tip 2: Unfortunately, there is a tendency toward eating disorders, particularly in girls, during middle and high school years. Whether their reasons include conforming to what they think they should look like or a desire to succeed at their sport, coaches need to be aware of this phenomenon. The worst thing a coach can do is to make weight a focal point for adolescent athletes. Weighing athletes at regular intervals, for instance, often causes or aids in the development of such disorders and should not be done.. For the very few sports that involve specific weight classes (like wrestling), coaches should promote wrestling in weight classes that are as close to the child's natural weight as possible.

Eating and Sleeping Habits

Although athletes this age enjoy generally good health, diet and sleeping habits often are poor.

Tip: Provide helpful advice on diet, specifically about the amount and kinds of food athletes should be eating before, during, and after practices and competitions. Also, sell your athletes on the fact that if they want to be successful, they must be disciplined and organized. Regular habits with regard to sleep, in addition to school, homework, and practice, must be factored into their daily schedule, as it is crucial for maintaining the alertness and energy needed to succeed throughout the day.

Cognitive Characteristics

More Logical, Versatile, and Flexible Thinking

Adolescents have a greater capacity for logical thought than when they were younger, though there are enormous individual variations.[1] Many are also now beginning to think abstractly, which allows them to examine complex issues such as politics, religion, and morality that were previously beyond their intellectual grasp. In essence, thinking has become more versatile and flexible, which helps young adolescents become more capable of understanding moral and ethical principles.[2]

Tip 1: Because athletes have grown intellectually and can think more logically, coaches can use their normal "adult" vocabulary and concepts without too much worry about the message getting through.

A more nuanced sense of right and wrong begins to emerge during these years, which can both help and hinder a coach when dealing with issues involving discipline. Flexibility in understanding helps athletes grasp more quickly and clearly *why* a coach handles things a certain way. On the other hand, with greater ability to think abstractly, the adolescent is more able to question the reasons for rules and to think about the complexities of a situation. Arbitrary authority is often challenged.

Tip 2: Athletes at this age are much more aware of fairness with respect to what is right. And despite their sometimes questioning of your decisions, they ultimately will follow your lead while having more respect for you *if* you set reasonable rules and defend them regardless of who violated them. Being fair and consistent when dealing with any and all situations will contribute to the development of stronger individual Coach-Athlete (C-A) relationships as well as an overall tighter, more positive team dynamic.

Executive Function (Planning, Impulse Control, Reasoning)

Making decisions and carrying them out ("executive functioning") is one of the most important functions of our brain. This requires paying attention to what is important and disregarding what is not, evaluating and prioritizing information, and organizing information and having search strategies to get additional information if needed. It also involves the ability to monitor performance and the flexibility to correct errors or change strategies and plans, as well as to follow through.[3] The prefrontal lobe of the brain, which is in charge of all of these activities, is almost like the conductor of an orchestra (i.e., the rest of the brain's parts). [4] As we've noted, executive functioning improves throughout childhood. New studies have revealed, however, that the prefrontal cortex is the last area of the brain to develop and that much of its development occurs during the teen years and even into young adulthood. *The teenager still has a long way to go before he or she has mature executive functioning.*[5] We now have research to back up what we have observed for a long time: that most teenagers, smart in so many ways, often show a lack of common sense. The same teenager who engaged you in a philosophical discussion after practice one day might be the same one who drank alcohol at a party, had pictures taken of him or her at said party, then found out that the photos were posted all over the Internet.

Tip 1: Goal setting and the time management, discipline, and overall planning skills required to realize those goals are keys to improvement and success in sports. They are all functions of conscious control, and an athlete's practicing these skills will automatically strengthen his or her brain's ability to perform such functions.

Tip 2: Knowing about the late evolution of conscious control should help coaches be more understanding of teenagers' often erratic and seemingly silly behavior at times, as well as realize and appreciate the added importance of promoting the development of those key skills.

Social Characteristics

Overview

Whereas puberty is the physical manifestation of the transition from childhood to adulthood, psychologists have pinpointed another major aspect of becoming an adult: the seeking out and development of one's identity. Who am I? What do I like? What do I believe? What do I want to be? And how do I fit in, at school, on my team, in this world? As an adolescent starts to discover answers to these questions, he begins to recognize a continuity and similarity in his own personality and beliefs. Role confusion occurs when a person gets mixed signals, or no answers at all, when exploring these questions.

Tip: Coaches should take the time to point out to athletes the gifts they possess (sports-related or otherwise) and the areas they show aptitude and capability for, *no matter what the athlete's age.* Having said that, the middle school years are usually the time children begin to wonder about their place in the world and their future. As their coach, you are in a fabulous position not only to discover what makes them special, but also to let them know the great things you see in them. And because you hold such a position of authority and importance in their life, *they will listen.*

Due to the large number of roles and positions necessary to make up a team, their participating on a team actually aids athletes in forging their own identity. Whether it is something specific ("I am a sprinter"; "I do my best in the big games") or general ("I am a hard worker"; "I am a leader") that they learn about themselves, ultimately, a clearer picture of their uniqueness and importance within the team structure tends to unfold. Team talks on the subject of team roles and how all are needed to achieve success are excellent opportunities for building overall team cohesiveness, but also for recognizing each member's unique and valuable identity within the group.

Self-Consciousness and Negative Nicknames

Puberty changes have a huge impact on adolescents, socially and emotionally. They often become quite self-conscious as they try to adjust to these changes.

Tip: It seems that all ages have their boy-girl comparison issues. For a younger athlete, it might be a strength issue. For adolescents it may be an appearance or size issue. Keep it simple: *For athletes of any age, you* should avoid drawing attention to their physical differences, whether they are boy-girl or same-sex comparisons. Especially avoid using nicknames that are tied in any way to appearance. An athlete may appear to go along with such a nickname while secretly hating it. Why? To be accepted by the group, or because the coach is the authority figure, in which case the athlete feels he or she has to accept the moniker. Oftentimes an athelete's receiving a nickname from a peer group can be far more accept-able to the athlete. Yet even there, if the nickname is hurtful, you, as coach, are in a position to at least discourage it. All this may seem like much ado about nothing, but for those few who are victimized by hurtful nicknames it's a very big deal. In addition, alienated team members tend to sap team unity. Therefore, it is everyone's best interest to discourage divisive words or actions, such as negative nicknames.

Peer Pressure

Early adolescents feel a strong need to conform, to belong, to be a part of the crowd. Their need to be a member of a peer group outside the family structure is greater at this time than at any other developmental stage. Cliques are common. Middle school youngsters generally lack confidence and are going through the early stages of finding and firming up their identity.

Tip: Your team is a haven for belonging, and because adolescents want so desperately to belong, being a part of a team is often far more impor-tant to a thirteen-year-old than to a seven-year-old. Also, keep in mind that as the athletes on your team build confidence as a result of improv-ing in their sport, they will be better able to deal with any issues of nega-tive peer pressure that may crop up beyond the team confines.

Rules

Peer groups have become the source of general rules of behavior, though the moral code learned from their parents still directs their ethical com-pass. Sometimes there is a conflict between peer and adult codes. Develop-ing a code of behavior is a move toward adult independence and therefore to be desired.

Tip: There are certain good reasons for the rules you set up, and early teens need, even want, guidance and rules to help them understand the boundaries of accepted behavior. Try not, however, to issue edicts where none are needed. It's best to keep the number of rules to a minimum, but make sure you enforce those immediately, evenly, and fairly. Early adolescents generally are bursting with the urge to express their individuality. By allowing some of that self-expression to come forth, by not hamstringing them with guidelines that mandate their every little move and twitch, you, as coach, will gain their trust and allegiance.

Emotional Characteristics

Overview

Early adolescents are often moody and unpredictable. This is due both to the tremendous biological changes taking place and the churning conflict within as these children attempt to "grow up." Though certain religions and cultures still practice "coming of age" rituals (such as bar and bat mitzvahs and quinceranos), in general our society does not have clear-cut rituals that denote when a child has crossed the line to adulthood. Hence, most adolescents in our society will begin the journey toward adulthood mainly by trial and error—by testing the boundaries within themselves as well as those imposed by the authority figures in their lives. Without a doubt, this important transition can be a confusing time.

Tip: Athletes of this age do not need to be confused any more than they already are. So take the confusion out. Be the authority figure each athlete needs and wants, but be a compassionate and understanding one. Above all, be consistent in your approach and treat each athlete as equal *and* special.

Changing Outlook toward Adults

By early adolescence, children begin to look at their parents and teachers more objectively.

Tip: Adults are no longer an automatic beneficiary of the child's blind obedience and respect. Increasingly, one has to earn it. Of course, if you are a coach of a multi-age team and have established a respectful relationship already, your athletes will tend to remain respectful and follow your lead willingly. In any event, the keys to gaining and maintaining command and respect include your displaying fairness (no favorites), consistency in how you treat them, a strong belief in their potential and abilities, and a total commitment to the importance of your activity, accompanied by your supreme effort to achieve the team's goals. They will follow that dynamic lead.

High School (ages 14–15 to 17–18)

Picture This: It is the local high school's big basketball game against its cross-town rival, and the stands are full of mostly fellow students, though there are many parents and other adult fans as well. For most of the teenagers in the crowd, it's another social night out, another event where teens can hang out with their buddies, and where peers can see and be seen. The game is nearing the end, and although many of the players on both benches have played very little, if at all, they are still clearly engaged in the game, yelling and cheering for their teammates. During a time out, the coach diagrams a play quickly and concisely, and the players seem to pick up on the coach's message immediately, without any need for repetition. After one botched play, the coach is seen dressing down one of the players. Yet the player merely nods his head, runs back into the action, and ten seconds later makes a beautiful pass to the team's center, who slams a dunk through the hoop. The crowd goes wild, and then the student section leads the crowd in a rousing cheer.

For the most part, adolescents have now had a chance to get used to the physical changes in themselves and their peers. Although girls will still tend to worry about their appearance and weight, and many boys will focus on becoming more buff, this period in their life can be characterized by increased confidence and comfort with who they have become. Where they are going in life is another question altogether, making their future a growing source of anxiety for many high school adolescents.

Physical Characteristics

Overview (Sex-Based Differences in Development)

By high school most girls have completed their growth and other puberty-related changes, and even late developing boys have at least begun such growth spurts and changes. Therefore, peer and class groups are more homogenous than in middle school in terms of height, weight, and general appearance. Now that adolescents have reached high school, their improvement patterns will also change. Up until this time, their athletic improvement had been partially growth-induced. But by the end of puberty, this powerful, natural booster rocket has pretty much run its course.

Tip 1: Puberty will end for most girls by their first couple of years in high school. As a result, they must rely on other factors, such as improving technique, increasing physical effort (higher intensity workouts), developing extra muscle through strength training, and the continued development of a stronger, more confident mind. There is definitely an art to helping females maintain self-confidence and motivation for the sport during this period in their lives. If some of your female athletes are getting discouraged at the slower pace of improvement, help them understand that while progress may come at a slower pace, there are still many ways to continue to improve, and that you are committed to helping them continue to progress.

Tip 2: For most boys it is a completely different story. Puberty's growth-inducing booster rocket is at its most powerful as most boys are entering high school. Therefore, coaches must often work hard to keep discouraged but able males who had not reached puberty during middle school interested in their sport during a period of slower improvement. For a coach to help late bloomers remain interested in a sport until they mature is of critical importance for the athlete, for once puberty begins, physically induced improvement alone often launches them into an incredible period of rapid improvement and greater success.

Cognitive Characteristics

Overview (Intellectual Capability)

During high school the average teenager has nearly reached maximum intellectual capability in most areas, though lack of experience limits knowledge and the ability to use it somewhat. Moreover, executive function skills are still emerging, making judgment sometimes unreliable.

Tip 1: The biggest mistake a high school coach can make is to talk down to the athlete, either in tone or content. Although coaches must make sure there is no question about who is in charge, they must be careful about communicating with their athletes in a respectful, mature fashion. As coach, don't try to play games with your athletes or pull the wool over their eyes. They will know in a flash whether you can be trusted or are trying to manipulate them. Be honest, explain thoroughly what you are trying to do, and follow through. They will without question appreciate your effort and candor, and will respect you more for it, which is so important when you are asking so much of them.

Tip 2: Despite the fact that your athletes are now almost full-grown physically, they still have a long way to go with regard to common sense. Yes, they'll mess up sometimes, which makes discipline and structure that much more vital, especially at this stage in their lives. However, the enforcement of rules should be applied in an unobtrusive, respectful way. Remember, anyone can be a tyrant. It takes emotional control as well as a love of your athletes and what you are doing to create an atmosphere that is demanding, yet supportive, and an experience that's special.

Social Characteristics

Overview

High school athletes have a far better sense of who they are than they did in middle school, yet most are still wrestling with aspects of their identity as well as their future.

Tip: Most of your athletes are fortunate in that they have firm identities at least as athletes. However, athletics will not factor into most teenagers' future vocational plans (with the exception of maintaining fitness and health, of course). Yes, some will become teachers and coaches, and a few might go on to professional sports. But the vast majority of those who play for you will eventually migrate to professions outside sports. And as they near the end of their high school years, many still don't know what they want to become. Therefore, as they get closer to making decisions involving further schooling and/or vocations, you are in a superb position to offer them insights about their capabilities and, in general, to encourage them and offer them counsel.

The peer group is at its apex of importance in adolescents' lives, and, in many ways, supercedes relationships with adults. They care deeply about how they are perceived by their peers, and may try out new styles, values, behaviors, and roles. They can get a temporary sense of identity through the group while they are forging their individual sense of self.[6]

Tip: Coaches and parents are actually more needed than ever as stable rule makers and limit-setters, as value upholders, advisors, guides, cheerleaders, and role models. In all these ways adults are able to foster good judgment and help children make a successful transition to adulthood.

Emotional Characteristics

Overview ("Neither Fish nor Fowl," neither child, nor adult)

As mentioned before, there are few clear dates, celebrations, or other rituals that confirm a child's passing into adulthood. In the United States, adolescents can obtain a license to drive at sixteen years of age and join the military at eighteen, yet not legally drink until twenty-one. On any given day, a teenager might drive to work after school to perform a job with major responsibilities similar to those of an adult, then come home and sleep under a roof where the rules and family norms aren't so different than when he or she was a younger child. Talk about confusing! Yet despite the role confusion our society imposes on us, adolescents in high school are clearly more secure than they were even a few years earlier. In general, self-esteem, which had been so high during the kindergarten and elementary school years, and then had taken such a hit during the middle school years, is once again on the rise.

Tip: Bits and pieces, events and key people, all gradually help shape and form a child's often uneven, yet sure progress toward adulthood. The more skilled adolescents are at *any one thing*, the more capable and confident they will tend to feel in general. For this reason alone, the program you offer your athletes is a huge positive factor in their lives. Focusing your athletes on their improvement, on their increased competency in a sport, will go a long way toward making them feel more worthy and more valuable.

▶ Summary Points ▶ ▶ ▶

- ▶ In middle school, athletes span the ages of ten to eleven through fourteen to fifteen. For high school, ages start from fourteen to fifteen and end at seventeen or eighteen.

- ▶ Each child developmental stage can be approached from four different aspects of development—physical, cognitive, social, and emotional.

- ▶ Puberty is the signature "happening" during adolescence and typically occurs for girls during the middle school years and for most boys near the end of middle school/beginning of high school. Differences in physical development are most dramatic during this time.

- ▶ During high school, boys and girls often take on responsibilities similar to an adult's, yet are often treated at school and at home like children. Despite such role confusion, high school students tend to be more secure than they were in middle school.

Notes

1. Healy, Jane, 103–104, states: "Intellectual growth during adolescence seems to depend on several factors: (1) inherited potential and timetable; (2) the quality of previous brain development in reception and association areas; (3) cultural expectations; (4) the amount and type of stimulation given by school and home; (5) a balance of support and challenge at home; (6) the child's own emotional strength and motivation to make sense out of new information and practice skills."
2. Amer. Acad. of Child & Adol. Psychiatry, 6–7.
3. Korkman, Kirk & Kemp, 11.
4. Goldberg, El Khonan, 21–26.
5. NIH
6. Berk, Laura, 624–625.

References for both Child Development Chapters

American Academy of Child and Adolescent Psychiatry. (1999) Your adolescent. New York: HarperCollins.

Barkley, Russell (1995) Taking charge of ADHD: The complete, authoritative guide for parents. New York: Guilford.

Berger, K. S. (2001) The developing person through the life span. 5th ed. New York: Worth.

Berk, Laura E. (1999) Infants, children, and adolescents. 3rd ed. Needham Heights, MA: Allyn and Bacon.

Duke, Marshall P., Nowicki, Stephen, and Martin, Elizabeth A. Teaching your child the language of social success. Atlanta: Peachtree. 1996

Dykema, Ravi (2006) "Don't talk to me now, I'm scanning for danger:" How your nervous system sabotages your ability to relate: An interview with Stephen Porges about his polyvagal theory. *Nexus, March/April 2006*, 30–35.

Erikson, Erik H. (1963) Childhood and society. 2nd ed. New York: Norton.

Giannetti Charlene C. and Sagarese, Margaret (2001) Cliques: 8 steps to help your child survive the social jungle. New York: Broadway Books.

Goldberg, El Khonon (2001) The executive brain: Frontal lobes and the civilized mind. New York: Oxford.

Greenspan, Stanley I. (1993) Playground politics: Understanding the emotional life of your school-age child. Reading, MA: Addison-Wesley

Greenspan, Stanley I. (1995) The challenging child: Understanding, raising, and enjoying the five "difficult" types of children. Reading, MA: Addison-Wesley

Harrison, Alexandra, M.D. (2006) Interview in March of 2006

Healy, Jane M. (1994) Your child's growing mind: a practical guide to brain development and learning from birth to adolescence. New York: Doubleday.

Iacoboni, Marco (2008) Mirroring People. New York: Farrar, Straus and Giroux.

Korkman, M., Kirk, U., and Kemp, S. (1998) NEPSY: A developmental neuropsychological assessment: Manual. San Antonio: The Psychological Corporation, Harcourt Brace + Co.

LeDoux, Joseph (1998) The emotional brain: the mysterious underpinnings of emotional life. New York: Simon and Schuster.

NIH publication No. 01-4929 (2001) Teenage brain: a work in progress.

Palombo, Joseph and Berenberg, Anne H. (1999) Working with parents of children with non-verbal learning disabilities: A conceptual and intervention model. In J. A. Incorvaia, B. S. Mark-Goldstein, & D. Tessmer (Eds.). *Understanding, diagnosing, and treating AD/HD in children and adolescents: An integrative approach.* Northvale, NJ: Aronson.

Palombo, Joseph (2006) Nonverbal learning disabilities: A clinical perspective. New York: Norton.

Porges, Stephen W. (2001) The polyvagal theory: phylogenetic substrates of a social nervous system. *International Journal of Psychophysiology, 42,* 123–146.

Solms, Mark and Turnbull, Oliver (2003) The Brain and the Inner World: An Introduction to the Neuroscience of Subjective Experience. New York: ? (I'll find out)

9

Working With Your Coaching Staff

Throughout this book we have focused on you as an improving coach, with advice on how to relate to, motivate, and teach your athletes. This chapter discusses some of the ins and outs of working with your fellow coaches, including how to become an effective head and assistant coach. Usually, if you are brand new to coaching, you will probably begin as an assistant, but after that, who knows? Some prefer to help out and let others lead the way, others become head coaches and remain in that capacity, while many go back and forth as the needs of the teams or their life situations dictate.

I began coaching as a helper with the youngest swimmers on our home-town team, then evolved to head coach of that team within three years. However, during the next ten years, I flipped back and forth between assistant and head (even co-head a couple times) as I passed through college and into the working world. Yes, if you love coaching children, you should do fine leading or assisting, but there are unique aspects to each role that should be recognized. Bottom line: No matter what role you take, you are a member of a team within a team, working together as effectively as possible for the betterment of your athletes.

Head Coach as Leader of the Staff

The head coach sets the tone. In addition to being the leader-by-position, the head coach drives the team's philosophy and direction. In this section we will discuss the steps to be taken when assembling a coaching staff, as well as review some of the many ways to communicate with, and educate, one's staff.

Assembling a Staff

Assuming that you are the coach in charge of the program and that your program is large or complex enough to be more than a one-person operation, you will need assistance. When you look for help, you are trying to find a person who works well with fellow coaches, who respects and cares for children, especially the age group or groups he or she will be working with, and who shares a compatible philosophy of coaching with you. It's easier to ascertain all of this when you know the candidate or have seen the candidate's coaching style and "way" with young athletes. That is why I would recommend vetting such known quantities first. However, if all those in your applicant pool are unknown to you, take certain steps that will minimize the chances of hiring a dud.

1. **Don't Marry a Resume**! Resumes are a decent starting point. They will give you some sense of the candidate's experience level and overall history, but cannot give you a window into his or her personality or interpersonal skills. When hiring, you'll be looking at whether the individual will work well with the rest of the staff, whether he or she is a leader, respects young people, and is a positive type. Therefore, though you may initially have to cull your crop of applicants by reviewing their resumes (assuming there are enough applicants to cull!), regard the interview process as a far more revealing and important step in the process.

2. **Prepare for the Interview Process: Is There a Fit? Before interviewing, prepare questions and talking points that reflect the objectives you've established for your program.** First, what is the candidate's mindset with regard to treating and working with young people? Second, is the candidate's philosophy of coaching similar enough to what you and your program espouse? Third, does this person have the personality, flexibility, passion, and willingness to learn and grow with the staff that defines a comrade-in-arms as opposed to a stick-in-the-mud? You can certainly learn a lot about coaching philosophy by asking relevant questions. But though you will be able to get some sense of candidates in a face-to-face interview, you can't *know* how they will operate as a coach

until you see them in action. Be aware of this limitation, do all you can in the interview to draw the candidate out, then, if possible . . .

3. **Watch the Candidate in Action.** If you can work it out, take the candidate to one of your practices and see how this individual interacts with your squad. Introduce the candidate to your team, ask the candidate to help with some drill or activity, and, in those and other ways, allow that person some face time with your athletes. A few seasons ago my club team, New Trier Swim Club, hired three new coaches. During the interview process (which involved all full-time staff), when I got the chance to spend time with the candidates I asked each candidate to perform some relatively low-pressure coaching function, such as helping me administer the prepared practice to a couple lanes for several minutes. Invariably I gained clues as to how effective the candidate would be by watching body language, listening to their interactions with the athletes, and the athletes' responses. Those small snapshots definitely helped me better size up the candidate.

4. **Contact the References.** Another way to get a look at the candidate's viability is by contacting references. Yes, those people will be some what biased toward the candidate. However, you can still obtain important clues into the essence of that candidate by talking with their references. For instance, if I was filling a coaching position that involved beginning eleven and twelve-year olds, I would ask how well the candidate connects with children of that particular age, in addition to other potentially revealing questions. The responses that references provide can help paint a clearer picture of the candidates.

Communication with Your Staff

Communication is, quite simply, vital for the consistent and successful operation of your staff. As much as possible, you want to be on the same page with your coaches, and they with each other, regarding philosophy, the technical side of teaching, and coaching duties. There are a number of ways you can establish good communication to make this happen.

1. **Pre-season and Early Season Preparative Meetings.** There's a lot to do before your season begins, and the work can be done in a variety of venues. Meetings at the office is one way, but so are scheduled "business dinners," or even scheduled staff time while at coaching seminars, picnics, and other kinds of events or group

activities. Regardless of the venue, when you bring your staff together to discuss the running of your organization, set a business-like tone. To not waste time; prepare an agenda, and use the meeting to inform, share ideas, and express your philosophy, the objective being that your team of coaches will become more educated, get more comfortable with each other, and better learn the role each will play during the season. There are differing opinions as to whether to discuss business at a social function, but if it's a coaches' social, be clear when the business portion of the event is about to commence. The goal is to educate your staff as to each coach's role in the smooth running of the team, and, in the process, forge a strong (and eventually synergistic) working relationship with them, and each of them with the others.

2. **In-Season Staff Meetings.** Make in-season staff meetings regular events (once a week if possible), prepare an agenda, and conduct meetings efficiently. You want such meetings to be productive—not pointless—and looked upon as helping inform and improve the staff.

3. **One-on-One Meetings.** One-on-one meetings offer more face time with your coaches, but in a different form. Sometimes it's relaxing in the office together, sometimes it's gabbing with each other between contests or practices. Any form it takes, one-on-one time with your assistants provides great opportunities to bring things up you might not in a group setting, or just to get to know your fellow coach on a more personal level. It's also a perfect opportunity to mentor those less-experienced coaches on your staff.

4. **E-Mails, Phone Calls, and Text Messages.** All are ways to maintain the lines of communication so that your staff stays as up-to-date and informed as possible.

Education of Your Staff

Coaches need to be aware of any changes concerning their day-to-day job. They also must stay abreast of the latest in their sport. In its various forms, continuing education is a must for maintaining and improving any youth sports organization.

1. **The Day-to-Day Functioning of the Club.** As mentioned earlier,

weekly staff meetings, as well as e-mails and other memos, should be adequate for keeping the staff current on the daily running of the organization. Though this form of education is obvious, don't underestimate its importance. For whether the communication is through the more structured channels of staff meetings or e-mails or just by spending lots of time around each other during a coaching day, effective day-to-day communication helps staff members better understand their jobs and how each of them fits into the successful operation of the organization.

2. **Staying Current with Your Sport.** One critical avenue to organizational improvement involves keeping abreast of your sport's latest research, breakthroughs, and teaching and training methods. Seminars, clinics, books, and videos are all ways to improve one's knowledge base while keeping current. Let's hope that your organization encourages such education by providing partial or full remuneration for books, seminar fees, and the like. If not, and if you are in a position to champion such support, do so.

3. **The Team "Way."** Especially with larger organizations, staff should have a general understanding about the established philosophy, methods, and vocabulary. Many clubs start with a "mission statement," which is their team philosophy stated in simple terms. Fleshing out that philosophy in terms of what will be emphasized, with what methods and vocabulary, and communicating that philosophy to your staff, is a key component of a successfully run organization. No matter how gifted your coaches are, without a real collective sense of where the coaching unit is going, confusion and lack of cohesion can ensue. Again, the best solution is to have the whole staff together often—at seminars, in meetings, at contests—watching, listening to, discussing, and reaching conclusions together.

4. **Mentoring.** Sometimes your being of assistance to a certain coach needs to go beyond the norm, especially coaches with little experience who can benefit from more personal guidance and direction. You will know them when you work with them. They often lack confidence, and spending extra time to discuss and show them successful coaching methods can increase their productivity immensely and quickly. Showing them how to behave in certain circumstances and while coaching athletes of certain ages or ability levels, discussing methods that might work better in such and such

a situation, or showing them how to create effective lesson plans are just some of the ways your mentoring can help inexperienced staff members.

The Role of Assistant Coach

Great assistant coaches are the unsung heroes of any team. Assistant coaches, depending on the sport, will *lead* (groups) more or less often, as well as *support* the head coach (providing an extra pair of eyes, relaying the head coach's directions, maintaining order, etc.). A great assistant—one who is trusted, respected, capable, knowledgeable, and loyal to the team—is invaluable. I have always felt that two coaches, head and assistant, working synergistically can accomplish an unbelievable amount more than what a single coach alone can achieve. Expand that concept to many assistants working together in a larger organization, and mountains can be moved.

However, the role of an assistant is far different than that of a head coach. He or she is not the leader of the organization, nor should he or she be viewed as such. Rather, the assistant must be expert at *facilitating,* whether it's facilitation of that day's practice, team rules, or team philosophy. This kind of role doesn't mean the assistant always follows instead of leads, or can't suggest new ideas or directions for the team. But the main role is that of helper, not driver, and, as such, it does involve a different mindset. Sometimes part of that mindset—the view of one's position and importance—gets skewed negatively ("I'm not critical to the team"), which can cause that coach's own motivation to decline. We will now flesh out the many ways an assistant can be useful. Those assistants who read the next couple pages should never again question their importance to the team, the organization, and to the children they coach.

Assistant Coaches at Practices and Contests

Assistant coaches have a range of duties to perform at practices and contests and should be prepared to play an active, supportive role with both the head coach and the athletes. Many of these duties are inherent in the assistant position, but a new, and enterprising, assistant coach might want to review them first with the head coach to ensure all efforts are synchronized to the program's objectives. By the way, many organizations are too large for the head coach to be in charge of every athlete. Lead coaches are therefore appointed to run some of the groups. In this section when we use the term "head coach", we are referring to lead coaches also. The following describe ways to be an effective assistant coach at practices and contests.

1. **Support the Team Philosophy.** You absolutely need to be a team player first! Mavericks, no matter how talented, can sow discord and dissension. Before you even sign on, know what the head coach believes in, how he or she operates, and what the team's mission statement is, because part of your job will be in promoting those things. You don't have to be on the same page always. However, if there are disagreements, bring them up in a diplomatic way. Otherwise, believe in and put your energy into what the team stands for, and in so doing, you will help create a positive, united, supportive staff. If you feel uncomfortable with any aspects of the program, seek a better fit with another organization.

   Note: There should be no real philosophical differences on how to handle the beginning program levels, such as Pee-Wee (five- to eight-year-old) soccer or Little League. For the very young, it's all about participating (action) and having fun while learning the rudiments of the sport, and as long as that basic philosophy holds, head and assistant coaches (many, if not most of them, being moms and dads) needn't worry about this issue. If, however, that beginning league promotes winning at all costs, for instance, then take your coaching efforts (and, if you are a parent, your child!) elsewhere.

2. **Support Whomever is Leading.** Actively support the leader of the group you are assisting—physically, verbally, and non-verbally, through body language. How do you go about it?

   • Be aware of when the leader asks for attention, and if your athletes aren't paying attention, help make sure they do.

   • When splitting up into smaller groups, try to use similar vocabulary to what the leader uses to explain what will be accomplished next, thus maintaining cohesion of thought and action.

   • Perform all tasks the best you can! You need to be a self-starter, a self-motivator. It can be easy to get bored and "check out" if you let yourself because, after all, someone else is running the show, so how important can *your* role be?! Quite crucial, as it turns out, and you have to believe it! *Know* you are important, a vital member of an integral team-teaching approach that relies on all doing their part. Do your very best, and you will not only raise the level of the total coaching team, but you will justifiably feel a stronger sense of satisfaction at how much you positively impacted your charges.

- Strive to know the athletes you are assisting as quickly and as well as possible. The stronger the C-A connection, the more you can know your athletes' capabilities and minds, resulting in better coaching and motivating. Also, the better you know them, the more effective you will be as their leader when placed in that position, as you will be from time to time.

- Anticipate! Be flexible and alert. At times, a good portion of an assistant's role (and value) is in anticipating what the head coach's or group's needs will be, and responding to such needs. For example: Two coaches are covering a swim practice, one on each side of the pool. As the head (or lead) coach moves from one side to the other to relay information to those swimmers who have just finished a set, an alert assistant will automatically shift to the other side of the pool to maintain visibility and connection with that half of the overall group. Or, take the same two coaches, same set up. But instead of shifting sides, the assistant might anticipate the finishing of the set, ask the head coach what to say to that group, then relay the information directly. These are two of many effective ways to handle such a situation. Think of practice as an ongoing drama or production, with hundreds of situations popping up continually. How can you contribute so that the production operates at a higher level? Fact is, at times you, as an assistant, will have no specific task during a portion of a practice or contest. Yet always remember—at the least, you are an extra pair of eyes, another crowd controller, another "expert." Therefore, if you have no specific task, *constantly look for ways to help make any practice or contest go better.*

There can only be one head coach, one main driving force on a team. Even if there are co-heads, there should be one vision, one mission statement that is promulgated by all. Otherwise disagreements over direction ensue, wasting time and energy. Therefore, to best create a united, smooth-functioning coaching team, assistants must support the head coach's game plan and overall team philosophy. Yet you, as assistant, are not a robot. You have a unique personality and capabilities that will leave their own positive mark on any you work with. As well, you have an opportunity to learn from fellow coaches and to grow with experience. Embrace your role as assistant and *know* that any successful organization needs great assistants to achieve their full potential.

▶ Summary Points ▶ ▶ ▶

▶ View the coaching staff as a team within a team.

▶ When selecting additions to the staff, make sure they possess a respect and caring for young athletes and that they share a similar coaching philosophy.

▶ Be thorough when vetting a prospective coach—demand (and thoroughly review) a resume, interview any serious candidates, observe, if possible, the candidate in action, and check the candidate's references.

▶ Maintaining consistent communication with your staff, including using e-mails, having regular staff meetings, and using one-on-ones and other opportunities, will keep everyone up-to-date on the program and ensure the ongoing, smooth functioning of the organization.

▶ Keep your staff current on the latest techniques, training, and other aspects of your sport by showing or recommending tapes and videos, by supporting involvement in clinics and seminars, and by recommending relevant books and articles.

▶ Operate with the view that great assistant coaches are truly the unsung heroes of any team!

▶ Supporting the head (or lead) coach in a variety of ways is an important role of an effective assistant. Help keep order, take attendance, and demonstrate techniques in practices. Because assistant coaches sometimes lead themselves, they should build strong C-A connections with the athletes they work with, and should *constantly* look for ways they can help practices or contests operate more successfully.

The Benefits of Participation in Age Group Sports

Why do parents sign up their children for age group sports programs? Often, the impetus comes from the child who may love the sport or who might be itching to do what an older sibling is doing. In addition, parents are usually on the lookout for programs that can do certain things, such as help their child build friendships and develop social skills by belonging to a group, or increase their child's physical activity, or find an activity he or she can experience some success in.

As for coaches, you might wonder how they view coaching in an age group sports program. As previously noted, coaches mostly view their job in a performance-oriented way. Their task, after all, is to improve their charges in a particular sport. But, in general, they are *baseball* and *tennis* and *fencing* coaches, not *life* coaches, or so the argument goes. However, the benefits of a well-run youth program can be so numerous and life-enhancing, that I encourage coaches who have the narrower more sports-specific view to re-think their job descriptions and embrace a broader vision of the many ways they can, and do, constructively influence young lives. At the same time, I hope parents who read this chapter will acquire a greater, better informed appreciation of the opportunities that age group sports provide their children, not just in the sports arena but in the all important social arena as well.

Immediate Beneficial Effects

Provided that the coach isn't an ogre, and that the sports group or team provides a reasonably supportive environment, a child's participation for even a few weeks can offer him or her immediate benefits. Let's take a look at a few of these.

Physical Activity on a Regular Basis

There is nothing like a little exertion to cause children to eat when they should, sleep more soundly, and feel better. It's a well-known fact that exercise helps our many bodily systems, such as the cardiovascular and digestive systems, to operate more efficiently. In addition, exercise releases endorphins, hormones released by the brain that help us feel calmer and happier and, in general, increase our feelings of well-being. Therefore, any sport that involves a healthy amount of running, jumping, swimming, or other strenuous activity will have a beneficial effect on both mind and body. In this day and age, when so much of a youngster's non-school time is either spent in front of a computer or TV, or is scheduled in other ways (piano, reading improvement, etc.—where has free play gone?), the value of regularly scheduled physical activity is magnified.

Instant Peer Group

If a child is new to an area or school, or if he doesn't have many playmates or friends who fit into his age or interest level, joining a team opens the door instantly to a group of similarly aged young ones who all have at least one interest in common—the sport. Friendships inevitably blossom. An exceptional example of how important joining a team can be occurs when a child in his or her early teens from a small middle school first enters the halls of that district's large high school. It is daunting to be one of the youngest among a thousand or more students! Joining a team, however, can help ease this feeling of alienation. It guarantees a peer group, a haven, a place and crowd that help the child feel that he or she belongs, potentially intimidating environment notwithstanding.

Confidence Building (Everyone Can Succeed at One or More Sports)

There is likely a sport for any child who has some combination of skills and motivation. A small and quick child with good coordination potentially may be an effective guard in basketball or lead-off hitter in baseball. Is the athlete big and perhaps heavy for his or her age? Most football linemen, shot putters, discuss throwers, and athletes competing in wrestling's higher weight classes come from this type. How about the diminutive child, yet with decent strength for his or her body weight? Wrestling, gymnastics, and ice-skating are three possibilities for such children. Perhaps the child does not demonstrate much athletic ability, but has great focus and a sharp eye? He or she may be a natural for archery. And what about the child who has yet to develop upper- body strength? Some of our best cross-country and distance runners fit this profile. Even youngsters who can't find their niche on land discover they are like fish when they hit the water! (My daughter was that way.) This, or course, opens up a whole host of water sports, including swimming, water polo, and synchronized swimming.

There is a sport or activity for most any child, and getting involved with the right one can do wonders for a child's self-confidence *right then*. And *that*, in turn, can have an immediate beneficial effect on their schoolwork, relations at home and at school, and in the continued building of self-esteem.

Acquiring Longer-Term Beneficial Habits

In addition to the many immediate benefits youth sports can provide, these activities can yield some impressive, longer-term rewards in the form of success habits learned and internalized if the child sticks with the program for an extended period of time. These habits can transfer to any area of a person's life. For example, the ability to efficiently manage one's time is of tremendous value in the business world (or, for that matter, in the operation of everyday life). The following are some of the most notable success habits acquired and reinforced through participation in age group sports.

The Relationship Between Effort and Progress

At first blush it seems obvious: Work hard and ye shall get better at whatever you are doing. The corollary would be: Work *harder*, and ye shall improve *faster*! Yet that simple equation can often elude a child for years, and some never embrace it. Why? Often children will notice their peers improving at a faster rate than they are, not realizing at the time that those peers also were *growing* at a faster rate or that there were other extenuating circumstances to explain improvement differences. However, once understood and internalized, the concept of improvement through focus and practice helps any youngster have a better chance at succeeding in life. Through organized sports, children learn *cause* ("I concentrated and tried real hard"), and the resultant *effect* ("I am improving *because* I focused and put out greater effort").

One of the first things children become aware of upon joining a team is that there are practices, often held on a regular basis, during which the athletes learn new skills and repeat over and over what they have learned. They come to realize that, in addition to improving themselves, practicing improves their team's chances of winning. However, it may take some time (and your encouragement) for them to understand and *really believe* that the greater the personal effort and focus, the speedier their progress. Why the delay for some? As mentioned earlier, uneven growth among peers, and the inability to see that such unevenness is occurring, is one reason. Another reason is that they see that some of their peers pick up the sport much faster and with more ease than they do. In other words, a young child's focus early on is about how she stacks up against her peers. "Why can't I be as good as she is? I try just as hard!" They are learning that talent is parceled out unevenly, but can't get beyond the fact that it is unfair. Eventually (and more quickly with your, the coach's, help) young athletes will develop the ability to measure improvement based on their own efforts—not by how they compare with others—and realize that it is the surest way to measure their individual improvement, and not by how they compare with others. Once the young athlete can focus on his or her own improvement, the lesson of "greater effort = faster improvement" will more readily take hold.

Another obstacle to an age group athlete understanding the importance of measuring improvement in terms of his or her own performance occurs during the first few months of the child's exposure to a sport, when the child is first trying to grasp *how to do the sport*, never mind improving!

When the total focus is on just trying to "get it," there is little thought given to "getting it" better and better.

An additional roadblock to ingraining this concept in young minds occurs when the coach or parents are too negative. A constant emphasis on what the athlete is doing wrong undermines the positive reinforcement of what he or she is doing correctly. Coaches of young athletes should always be on the watch for effort and subsequent improvement. Then it's important to make that connection for the athlete. For example: "You came to practice four times last week instead of the two times you normally attend. And you really concentrated. That's why you just performed your best ever!" Eventually the athlete will grasp the concept, then embrace it more and more as he or she comes to understand how central the concept is to the speed of evolution in that sport and ultimately toward achieving success in anything they choose to pursue. And even though, being human, athletes may not want to put a maximum effort into practice all the time ("Work is hard!"), they will have ingrained a success habit they can use anytime when they really want to achieve something.

Time Management

Humans can be incredibly productive when they learn how to plan ahead. By the time athletes reach high school, for instance, they need to organize their days to the minute if they are to jam in time for classes, homework, and the now- longer practice hours required of them. Social time can be scarce, so the team fills that void. While achieving acceptable grades and excelling at a sport may seem daunting at first, the majority of students who take on a sport actually do better in class than those with extra time on their hands. Most of the credit for this phenomenon goes to the fact that, if athletes want to succeed, in school and at their sport, they *must* become organized in their time use, or they will have difficulties in one or both. Younger athletes don't tend to have as much asked of them, either at school or on the field. Yet this success habit starts developing in junior high or even earlier, as school and activities force them to make choices about how they will allocate their time and for what.

Goal Setting and Problem Solving

To wish for a certain thing, or to want to become a certain somebody (say, a fireman or singer), is what captures every child's imagination at one time or another. Yet how to get there? The object of that *want* remains elusive, vague, unreachable—seeming, to be merely a wish. Why? Because there is no concrete plan for attaining that objective. No specific blueprint for the best way in which to gain whatever it is that youngster desires. It's kind of like traveling without a map. Learning to set realistic goals—short, inter- mediate, and long-term goals—gives our efforts direction and focus. It is akin to finding a roadmap and plotting a course. It makes the unbelievable believable. The key to taking on any major challenge and succeeding is to break it down into several plausible objectives. Achieving each of the series of realistic objectives will have, as an end result, the attainment of the major goal.

Children learn how to set goals in athletics. In essence, they learn how to problem-solve by breaking down major challenges into simpler, do-able parts. Of course, an equally important aspect to goal setting is to *commit* to accomplishing said goals. That's the effort part. However, the ability to establish intelligent objectives comes first; then, commitment firms up when one becomes clear about how to reach the objective. Throw in hard work and focus—presto! Seemingly insurmountable challenges are achieved, new goals set, and a heck of a lot is accomplished. Science proj- ects, math problems, chores at home, all become easier to understand and accomplish. When youngsters grasp the concept, then succeed at realizing their objectives, you better believe their confidence in being able to start and finish *whatever* they sets their sights on will blossom.

Teamwork and Sacrifice

Being involved in a team sport teaches that, through cooperation, the whole group benefits. Basketball players learn to appreciate that good passing and rebounding are just as important as sinking shots. Wrestlers of different weights help each other learn on the practice mat because they realize that success in all weight classes is critical for a winning team score. And that elusive thing called "team chemistry" we hear about so much is actually nothing more than players pulling for each other and helping each other out—with no strings attached. *Unconditional support.* Everyone working together for the greater good. And as mentioned in the chapter on teamwork, even five- and six- year-olds who are still mainly egocentric can begin to understand the concept by watching their older teammates in a multi-age sport such as swimming, (age group swim teams often have six- and sixteen-year-olds on the same team), or older athletes, who are one or more levels ahead, in a program such as soccer or Little League.

Once young athletes buy into the concept of teamwork, they will become more able to understand sacrifice, and to more readily "take one for the team" when necessary. A softball player who has been "pinch-hit" for may not like it, but she will still understand that the manager feels it's best for the team to replace her with another batter. A soccer mid-fielder may be asked to play fullback one game because the defense is weak and he is the best all-around player the team has. He may not be ecstatic with the decision, but he accepts the change, and therefore sacrifices his own wishes for the greater good of the team.

Learning to be a team player will reap huge dividends as the child grows up. Whether in a high school play, in a college group project, or in any business where teamwork is necessary (not to mention within the family!), teambuilding, sacrifice for the greater good, and other team-oriented skills will be of tremendous value.

Sportsmanship

Sportsmanship is an unwritten code of conduct that promotes fair play and an appreciation for the efforts of the others involved, including teammates, opponents, and officials. Respect for others is at the root of good sportsmanship. To be gracious in victory as well as in defeat, to play to the best of one's abilities within the rules, and to congratulate one's opponent sincerely for their efforts are all demonstrations of fine sportsmanship.

On the field of play, learning and practicing good sportsmanship means that children are developing positive people skills—that is, emotional intelligence. The more developed their emotional intelligence, the happier and more effective they can be in their dealings with others throughout their lives.

A coach's role in teaching character and sportsmanship cannot be underestimated. Children who are at the beginning of their physical development as athletes are emotionally young as well, and they must be taught and reinforced about what's right and how to handle situations correctly. As an example, a seven-year-old swimmer may feel like throwing his goggles in disappointment after a subpar race because he feels unhappy about the outcome. He hasn't yet developed a method for handling those negative emotions, and out they come! A coach can show the child how to more constructively channel his disappointment while pointing out a different, more constructive way for the child to view his performance. But, and this is crucial, *the coach's actions must conform to what he or she teaches.* The coach cannot, on the one hand, espouse respect for the officials, then berate them during a game! In this case, mixed messages will result in a sense among the athletes that it is okay to *not* be respectful. ("Coach did it, so it's okay"). A coach's consistent teaching and modeling of sportsmanship will help give each athlete a solid foundation for treating people with respect. Where else can a young person experience such a number of competitive situations, and be mentored and learn through those experiences, as in youth sports?

Positive Self-Esteem

In the final analysis, a successful youth sports experience isn't so much about achieving excellence in any particular sport. Rather, it is that through that experience children acquire and reinforce positive life habits that translate into success in life. Children discover they can do far more than they thought by developing the ability to set and achieve goals through great effort, managing their time efficiently, and working harmoniously with their peers. They therefore have developed self-reliance, the certainty that they can accept and conquer challenges of all types *by themselves.* Consequently, their self-esteem, their ability to like and value themselves, rises across the board. I have lost count of the number of parents who have gone out of their way to tell me how their formerly struggling child is suddenly surging in school as a result of the success he or she experienced, and the confidence he or she gained, by participating in our swim program. Countless business, religious, educational, and community leaders will tell you that their own positive self-esteem development was given a critical boost through participation in youth sports. The life lessons they internalized during those formative years contributed to their subsequent success. The fact is that we are all far more able to successfully handle the ups and downs of our daily existence when we develop the confidence that, by keeping at it, by never giving up, by constantly searching for a way, we will emerge victorious. Lance Armstrong, the seven-time Tour de France winning cyclist, when asked how he went about dealing with his severe bout of testicular cancer that eventually reached his brain, replied, "I approached cancer the way I would prepare for the Tour [de France]. Get in shape, find out as much as I can, be motivated by small results."

How can coaches help build self-esteem? There are three major aspects to being successful in doing this.

1. We need to teach positive success habits such as goal setting and teamwork.

2. We must provide positive feedback when our athletes do something correctly.

3. We must promote and reinforce the truth about how they are doing.

We must understand, that we are actually doing harm if, for instance, we tell our athletes they are doing skills correctly when they aren't. Of course, coaches want to be encouraging, especially to younger, more novice athletes who are less certain of their capabilities. But making false observations is not the way. *Part of the art of coaching in this type of situation is in telling the truth in such a way that the athlete becomes more motivated, not less.* Take an example from hockey: *Don't say:* "That's the best slap shot I've ever seen!" when what you mean is, "It's obvious you have been working on your slap shot. Your wrist action is far more powerful than before." Actually, every once in awhile we do see a young athletes perform better than they ever have before. In that type of situation, it would be both motivational and truthful to say "That's the best slap shot I have ever seen *you* perform!" Every so often, I make such an observation to this or that athlete, and it never fails to result in a re-doubling of effort. The key is that all observations be based on what's actually happening, and not on some fiction that will temporarily (and falsely) make the athlete feel good.

What we have discussed here are just some of the short- and long-term benefits of participation in youth sports, and the fact that so much of what athletes learn and experience have far-reaching implications for their overall growth should argue convincingly for the "big picture" view of coaching. We have an incredible opportunity to help build the person, not just the athlete, and the more we embrace this view, the more rewarding our athletes' experiences will be.

▶ Summary Points ▶ ▶ ▶

▶ The benefits of participation in age group sports go far beyond improvement in any particular sport.

▶ Some immediate beneficial effects include having physical activity on a regular basis, joining and then belonging to a group whose members all have at least one major interest in common, and building positive self-esteem through improvement and success for any child in any given sport. Long-term success habits that are acquired through participation in sports include: developing an understanding and belief in the relationship between hard work and progress, greater time management capability, an improved ability to goal-set and problem-solve, the ability to work together as a team, and the learning and exhibiting of sportsmanship.

▶ Coaches can help build self-esteem in athletes in three important ways—emphasize positive success habits, provide positive feedback when something is done correctly, and always promote and reinforce the truth about about an athlete's improvement development and performance.

Index

Racom Communications Order Form

QUANTITY	TITLE	PRICE	AMOUNT
_____	The Art of Coaching Young Athletes, **Pick Peterson**	$19.95	_____
_____	The *IMC Handbook*, **J. Stephen Kelly/Susan K. Jones**	$49.95	_____
_____	Creative Strategy in Direct & Interactive Marketing, 4th Ed., **Susan K. Jones**	$49.95	_____
_____	Innovating . . . Chcago Style, **Thomas Kuczmarski, Luke Tanen, Dan Miller**	$27.95	_____
_____	The New Media Driver's License, **Richard Cole/Derek Mehraban**	$24.95	_____
_____	Aligned, **Maurice Parisien**	$24.95	_____
_____	How to Jump-Start Your Career, **Robert L. Hemmings**	$19.95	_____
_____	This Year a Pogo Stick . . . Next Year a Unicycle!, **Jim Kobs**	$19.95	_____
_____	Follow That Customer, **Egbert Jan van Bel/Ed Sander/Alan Weber**	$39.95	_____
_____	Internet Marketing, **Herschell Gordon Lewis**	$19.95	_____
_____	Reliability Rules, **Don Schultz/Reg Price**	$34.95	_____
_____	The Marketing Performance Measurement Toolkit, **David M. Raab**	$39.95	_____
_____	Successful E-Mail Marketing Strategies, **Arthur M. Hughes/Arthur Sweetser**	$49.95	_____
_____	Managing Your Business Data, **Theresa Kushner/Maria Villar**	$32.95	_____
_____	Media Strategy and Planning Workbook, **DL Dickinson**	$24.95	_____
_____	Marketing Metrics in Action, **Laura Patterson**	$24.95	_____
_____	Print Matters, **Randall Hines/Robert Lauterborn**	$27.95	_____
_____	The Business of Database Marketing, **Richard N. Tooker**	$49.95	_____
_____	Customer Churn, Retention, and Profitability, **Arthur Middleton Hughes**	$44.95	_____
_____	Data-Driven Business Models, **Alan Weber**	$49.95	_____
_____	Branding Iron, **Charlie Hughes and William Jeanes**	$27.95	_____
_____	Managing Sales Leads and Sales & Marketing 365, **James Obermayer**	$56.95	_____
_____	Creating the Marketing Experience, **Joe Marconi**	$49.95	_____
_____	Coming to Concurrence, **J. Walker Smith/Ann Clurman/Craig Wood**	$34.95	_____
_____	Brand Babble, **Don E. Schultz/Heidi F. Schultz**	$24.95	_____
_____	The New Marketing Conversation, **Donna Baier Stein/Alexandra MacAaron**	$34.95	_____
_____	Trade Show and Event Marketing, **Ruth Stevens**	$59.95	_____
_____	Accountable Marketing, **Peter J. Rosenwald**	$59.95	_____
_____	Contemporary Database Marketing, **Martin Baier/Kurtis Ruf/G. Chakraborty**	$89.95	_____
_____	Catalog Strategist's Toolkit, **Katie Muldoon**	$59.95	_____
_____	Marketing Convergence, **Susan K. Jones/Ted Spiegel**	$34.95	_____
_____	High-Performance Interactive Marketing, **Christopher Ryan**	$39.95	_____
_____	Public Relations: The Complete Guide, **Joe Marconi**	$49.95	_____
_____	The Marketer's Guide to Public Relations, **Thomas L. Harris/Patricia T. Whalen**	$39.95	_____
_____	The White Paper Marketing Handbook, **Robert W. Bly**	$39.95	_____
_____	Business-to-Business Marketing Research, **Martin Block/Tamara Block**	$69.95	_____
_____	Hot Appeals or Burnt Offerings, **Herschell Gordon Lewis**	$24.95	_____
_____	On the Art of Writing Copy, **Herschell Gordon Lewis**	$34.95	_____
_____	Open Me Now, **Herschell Gordon Lewis**	$21.95	_____
_____	Marketing Mayhem, **Herschell Gordon Lewis**	$39.95	_____
_____	Asinine Advertising, **Herschell Gordon Lewis**	$22.95	_____
_____	The Ultimate Guide To Purchasing Website, Video, Print & Other Creative Services, **Bobbi Balderman**	$18.95	_____

Name/Title_____

Company _____

Street Address _____

City/State/Zip _____

Email _____ Phone _____

Credit Card: ☐ VISA ☐ MasterCard
              ☐ American Express ☐ Discover

☐ Check or money order enclosed (payable to Racom
   Communications in US dollars drawn on a US bank)

Number _____ Exp. Date _____

Signature _____

Subtotal	_____
Subtotal from other side	_____
8.65% Tax	_____
Shipping & Handling	_____
$7.00 for first book; $1.00 for each additional book.	
TOTAL	_____

Racom Communications, 150 N. Michigan Ave, Suite 2800, Chicago, IL 60601
312-494-0100, 800-247-6553, www. Racombooks.com